WHY
MOTIVATING
PEOPLE
DOESN'T
WORK . . .
AND
WHAT DOES

WHY MOTIVATING PEOPLE DOESN'T WORK . . . AND WHAT DOES

More Breakthroughs for Leading, Energizing, and Engaging

SECOND EDITION

SUSAN FOWLER

Berrett–Koehler Publishers, Inc.

Berrett-Koehler Publishers, Inc.
1333 Broadway, Suite 1000
Oakland, CA 94612-1921
Tel: (510) 817-2277
Fax: (510) 817-2278
www.bkconnection.com

ORDERING INFORMATION
Quantity sales. Special discounts are available on quantity purchases by corporations, associations, and others. For details, contact the "Special Sales Department" at the Berrett-Koehler address above.
Individual sales. Berrett-Koehler publications are available through most bookstores. They can also be ordered directly from Berrett-Koehler: Tel: (800) 929-2929; Fax: (802) 864-7626; www.bkconnection.com.
Orders for college textbook / course adoption use. Please contact Berrett-Koehler: Tel: (800) 929-2929; Fax: (802) 864-7626.

Distributed to the U.S. trade and internationally by Penguin Random House Publisher Services.

Berrett-Koehler and the BK logo are registered trademarks of Berrett-Koehler Publishers, Inc.

Printed in the United States of America

Berrett-Koehler books are printed on long lasting acid-free paper. When it is available, we choose paper that has been manufactured by environmentally responsible processes. These may include using trees grown in sustainable forests, incorporating recycled paper, minimizing chlorine in bleaching, or recycling the energy produced at the paper mill.

Library of Congress Cataloging-in-Publication Data

Names: Fowler, Susan, 1951- author.
Title: Why motivating people doesn't work ... and what does : more
  breakthroughs for leading, energizing, and engaging / Susan Fowler.
Description: Second edition. | Oakland, CA : Berrett-Koehler Publishers,
  Inc., [2023] | Includes bibliographical references and index.
Identifiers: LCCN 2022049280 (print) | LCCN 2022049281 (ebook) | ISBN
  9781523004126 (paperback ; alk. paper) | ISBN 9781523004133 (pdf) | ISBN
  9781523004140 (epub) | ISBN 9781523004157 (audio)
Subjects: LCSH: Employee motivation. | Leadership.
Classification: LCC HF5549.5.M63 F69 2023 (print) | LCC HF5549.5.M63
  (ebook) | DDC 658.3/14—dc23/eng/20221012
LC record available at https://lccn.loc.gov/2022049280
LC ebook record available at https://lccn.loc.gov/2022049281

Second Edition
30 29 28 27 26 25 24   10 9 8 7 6 5 4 3 2
Interior design: Reider Books
Cover design: Frances Baca
Copyediting: PeopleSpeak

For Drea

Contents

Foreword

by Garry Ridge

When I stepped down as CEO after twenty-five years, I handed over the secret formula to WD-40's Multi-Use Product to a new era of leadership. During that time, our water-displacement lubricant in the blue and yellow cans with the little red top called WD-40 emerged as one of the most recognizable household items in the world. Warren Buffet regards it as a brand with one of the best competitive moats on the planet.[1]

Most people assume that WD-40's success is its secret formula. And they are right. But I believe it's our other secret formula that guided us to a market cap that's grown from $300 million to $2.5 billion and exceeded the performance of the Russell 2000 and S&P by a long shot, delivering a shareholder return of 1,369 percent without laying off a single person in hard economic times or during the COVID-19 pandemic. What is the other secret formula? WD-40 is fueled by an optimally motivated workforce demonstrated through our people's spirit, morale, inspiration, commitment, and desire to use their discretionary effort on behalf of our company.

It seems impossible that there is anyone left in the world who still needs convincing that a people-first culture is essential to the long-term success of any company. In the good years and the not-so-good years, it is the spirit of our people that makes us great. But we animated our hidden secret by building an inclusive and diverse, learning and teaching, and purposeful organization where our people succeed together while excelling as individuals. Some see human capital as an expense. We see our people, our tribe, as the essence of our organization. Our success comes from nurturing people's optimal motivation and engagement.

That's where Susan's work comes in. I first met Susan in 2001 when I decided to earn my master of science in executive leadership from the University of San Diego. She and her husband, Dr. Drea Zigarmi, taught the first week of the twenty-two-month program. Susan's research on motivation science was in its early stages. For the past twenty years, she has refined her approach and the Spectrum of Motivation® model with thousands of leaders from organizations in over forty countries.

Dozens of WD-40 Company executives have participated in the master's program, learning to master motivation for themselves and others. WD-40 Company's special formula for success aligns with what motivation science proves: the optimal motivation required for people to thrive and produce quality results comes from fulfilling people's three psychological needs.

WD-40 Company's Special Formula for Success

Our job as leaders is to make sure we create an environment where our tribe members wake up each day inspired to go to work, feel safe while they are there, and return home at the end of the day fulfilled by the work that they do, feeling that they have learned something new and contributed to something bigger than themselves. At WD-40 Company, we do that in three ways:

We encourage choice. We promote autonomy by helping people move from fear to freedom. We eliminated one of the greatest fears—the fear of failure. People do not fail at WD-40 Company; they have learning moments. We define a learning moment as a positive or negative outcome of any situation that needs to be openly and freely shared among the tribe. We celebrate learning moments.

We deepen connection. I'm convinced that the heart of our success is built on a culture of belonging. Our culture reflects a self-sustaining and interdependent tribe where members share common attributes such as values, knowledge, celebration, ceremony, and a strong sense of belonging. Belonging is not all "kumbaya." It is a balance between being tough-minded and tenderhearted—where people feel safe and able to do their best work.

When other companies were experiencing the Great Resignation starting in 2020 (I really think it was the Great Escape from toxic cultures), our employee engagement average remained at 93 percent, including 98 percent reporting excitement about the company's future. If we had employee engagement like most companies have, we would need twice as many people to do the same job, which means that we would not have the financial results we have today.

We build competence. Our company focuses on learning moments, encouraging tribe members to try something new, ask for help, and learn from their experiences. But we also proactively build people's competence through peer coaching. Every leader is also a coach, responsible for promoting people's growth.

We know motivating people doesn't work, but we've figured out what does. I've witnessed firsthand how Susan's work, captured in this book, teaches you how to create a space where your tribe members will flourish. It takes dedication to create that safe playing field where people experience choice by moving from fear to freedom, connection through relationships protected by values and inspired by vision, and competence gained from learning moments. But it also takes skill based on a framework capturing the truth about human motivation and proven strategies leaders can apply daily so people can be the next version of their best selves.

Garry Ridge currently serves as chairman emeritus of WD-40 Company and coaches executives on how to lead a culture focused on people, purpose, passion, and product through his company, the Learning Moment.

Stop Beating Your People with Carrots

A funny thing happened on the way to understanding human motivation. Psychologists decided to study animals. For example, you can watch Harvard psychology professor B. F. Skinner on YouTube showing how he motivates a conditioned pigeon to do a 360-degree turn by rewarding its behavior with pellets. It is fascinating to watch as he rewards the bird for doing what he wants it to do—he can get it to do almost anything. Behaviorists reasoned that this method could motivate people in the workplace the same way: reward people for doing what you want them to do, and you can get them to do almost anything. And guess what? It worked—or seemed to. I call it the Pecking Pigeon Paradigm.

Using metaphorical pellets as incentives to motivate people to do tasks they don't necessarily want to do has become common practice. A massive industry exists to sell and support complex schemes for motivating workers with compensation systems, rewards, contests, tokens, badges, prizes, and formal recognition programs. Pellets and more pellets.

Irrefutable evidence demonstrates the futility of the Pecking Pigeon Paradigm. In thousands of experiments worldwide, the results are the same: even though people will take the money or rewards you offer, the only correlation between those incentives and performance is a negative one. In other words, external rewards produce a disturbing undermining effect on the energy, vitality, and sense of positive well-being people need to achieve goals, attain excellence, and sustain effort.[1]

Traditional forms of motivation may appear to work in some types of jobs or industries. For example, if you promise people more pellets, they may produce more on the assembly line in the short term. However, it is unwise to confuse productivity with thriving and flourishing. Without thriving and flourishing, short-term gains tend to turn into long-term opportunity losses. The Pecking Pigeon Paradigm never worked the way we thought it would—no matter the type of job or industry. The simple fact is, people are not pigeons.

This book offers plenty of proof that motivating people doesn't work. But the benefit for you—and my primary focus—is an empirically based and globally field-tested approach to developing your leadership capacity so you can take advantage of good science.

We Have Learned How to Put the Science to Work

Valid scientific and academic research requires four to six decades to make it into mainstream awareness. In the 1960s, the early appearances of the Self-Determination Theory (SDT) proposed by Dr. Edward Deci and Dr. Richard Ryan were considered provocative. Now you find nearly universal support for SDT, thanks to Deci and Ryan's dedication to a layered and thoughtful methodology, groundbreaking research supported by thousands of dedicated researchers around the world, and bestselling books by Alfie Kohn, Daniel Pink, and yours truly.[2] This elegant and complex theory is now firmly established at the perimeter of mainstream consciousness.[3]

My aim for the past twenty years has been to understand, translate, and apply the best motivation science to improve the quality of our lives, personally and professionally. Oliver Wendell Holmes allegedly said he didn't give a fig for the simplicity that lies on this side of complexity. So I've strived for the simplicity that lies on the other side of complexity.

We've come a long way toward gaining that higher level of simplicity since the original 2014 version of *Why Motivating People Doesn't Work . . . and What Does* became a bestseller and was translated into fourteen languages.

This second edition benefits from years of application and feedback, a refinement of language and processes, and new success stories. I have had the privilege of traveling around the world refining the Spectrum of Motivation model, testing the skill of motivation, and developing the three leadership capacities that encourage choice, deepen connection, and build competence. I started Mojo Moments®, a company with dozens of global partners dedicated to teaching the skill of motivation to leaders at all levels in the organization. This edition also benefits from recent research revealing what we learned about motivation during the COVID-19 pandemic years.

If you read the original book, you'll notice a change in language and the introduction of new terms. For example, the academic terms for the three basic psychological needs, *autonomy*, *relatedness*, and *competence* (affectionately referred to as ARC) are now *choice*, *connection*, and *competence* (with the blessing of Deci and Ryan, by the way).

You Still Need to Ask the Right Question

Are you motivated to read this book? You might find this a strange question given that you have already read this far. I agree it is silly but perhaps for a different reason.

Asking if you are motivated raises more questions than answers. What criteria do you use to determine whether you are motivated? If I asked you to decide whether a colleague of yours is motivated to read this book, how would you reach your conclusion? How do you evaluate another person's motivation? What does *motivation* even mean?

For many years, my go-to definition of motivation was simply "the energy to act." It turns out my definition has the same fatal flaw as the other 102 definitions you can find for motivation.[4] Thinking of being motivated as having the energy or impetus to act fails to convey the essential nature of human motivation. It does nothing to help you understand the reasons behind the action.

Asking if you are motivated to read this book is simply the wrong question. What if I asked instead, *Why* are you motivated to read this book? I might discover that you are reading this because you take being a leader seriously and you are struggling with the motivation of a staff member. You are hoping this book might shed light on your motivation dilemma.

Or I might discover that you are reading it because the head of your department told you to read it and you're afraid of what might happen if you don't. These two very different reasons for being motivated generate different qualities of energy. Instead of asking if you are motivated, I need to ask a different question to reveal your *reasons* for acting.

An important truth emerges when you explore the nature of motivation: people are always motivated. The question is not *if* but *why* they are motivated.

The motivation—or energy and impetus—a person brings to any action can be *qualitatively* different. Some reasons people are motivated tend to promote well-being for others and themselves—and unfortunately, some reasons don't:

- Motivation that comes from *choosing* to do something is different from motivation that comes from *having* to do it.
- Motivation generated from values, purpose, love, joy, or compassion is different from motivation generated from ego, power, status, or a desire for external rewards.
- Motivation to compete because of a desire to excel (where the score serves as feedback on how successfully you are growing, learning, and executing) is different from the motivation to compete to best someone else, impress, or gain favors.

One of the primary reasons motivating people doesn't work is our naïve assumption that motivation is something a person has or doesn't have. This leads to the erroneous conclusion that the more motivation a person has, the more likely she will achieve her goals and be successful. When it comes to motivation, assuming that more is better is too simplistic and even unwise. Motivation is similar to friendship: it doesn't matter how many friends you have but rather the quality and types of friendships.[5]

Imagine you are a sales manager. You wonder if your sales reps are motivated. You look at the midquarter sales reports for your two highest-selling reps and conclude, yes, they are both highly motivated. What you might fail to notice is that they are motivated differently. The reason one rep works hard is to win the sales contest, be seen as number one, and make the promised bonus. The reason the other rep works hard is that he values your products and services, his efforts are connected to a noble purpose, and he enjoys problem-solving with his clients. The science of motivation provides compelling evidence that the reps' different types of motivation have major implications. The quality of their energy affects short-term results and long-term stamina.[6]

Traditional motivation prompts the wrong questions: Is this person motivated? How much motivation does this person have? These questions reduce your answers to simplistic black-and-white, yes-or-no responses that fail to provide much-needed insight into the nature of the motivation.

But asking why a person is motivated leads to six empirically proven motivational possibilities. Appreciating these possibilities and the implications behind each of them enables you to take advantage of the Spectrum of Motivation model and guide your people to optimal and high-quality motivation.

From Theory to Practice

Motivating people doesn't work, but this book provides you with a framework, model, and powerful course of action that does.

Chapter 1, "The Motivation Dilemma," explains why you likely feel frustrated trying to motivate people. You've been held accountable for attempting the impossible: to motivate the people you lead. You will discover the Spectrum of Motivation model, which captures the chasm between outdated approaches that depend on motivational junk food and empirically proven alternatives that offer motivational health food.

Chapter 2, "What Motivates People: The Real Story," reveals the greatest breakthrough in motivation science—the psychological needs required for human thriving. You will learn the true nature of human motivation, the benefits of tapping into it, and the hidden costs of continuing to ignore it.

Chapter 3, "Shifting Out of Overdrive," presents alternatives to driving for results that, ironically, lead to better results. You'll learn the significance of self-regulation in people's motivation—and your role in helping them experience high-quality self-regulation.

Chapter 4, "If Motivating People Doesn't Work . . . What Does?," introduces a fresh and much-needed new vocabulary and set of skills for motivational leadership. Instead of outdated leadership competencies that are focused on driving for results or incentivizing behavior, you'll learn three new leadership capacities that encourage choice, deepen connection, and build competence to generate productivity without compromising vitality and well-being for the people you lead.

Chapter 5, "Rethinking Leadership Now That Everything Else Has Changed," applies leadership capacities to thorny issues such as managing a hybrid workforce. You also learn a new concept called *psychological sense* and how your leadership can improve people's ability to experience optimal motivation.

Chapter 6, "Leader, Heal Thyself," shares the stories of exemplary leaders who realized that mastering their own motivation provided a breakthrough for applying their leadership capacities to effectively lead others.

Chapter 7, "Are Your Beliefs Eroding People's Optimal Motivation?," challenges you to reconsider your own beliefs about motivation. For example, can you complete these common sayings?

- It's not personal; it's just _____.
- The purpose of business is to _____.
- Leaders are in a position of _____.
- The only thing that really matters is _____.
- If you cannot measure it, it _____.

These beliefs are so embedded in our collective psyche that you probably don't even need to check your answers. (But if you are curious, you can take a peek at chapter 7, which is dedicated to exploring these beliefs, where they come from, and if they still serve you, your people, and your outcomes.)

Chapter 8, "The Promise of Optimal Motivation," examines the potential of this fresh approach to motivation from three perspectives: the organization, the people you lead, and yourself.

Admitting that many traditional approaches to motivation have been counterproductive—or worse, destructive—frees us up for new ways of looking at motivation. We need to realize that applying pressure to achieve results has undermined the outcomes we were seeking. We need to consider that promoting contests and competitions for the sake of winning is not the best way to encourage and sustain performance. We need to appreciate that—despite the practical need for money and people's incessant requests for more—the focus on monetary rewards has obscured what truly satisfies people in their jobs. It appears motivating people doesn't work to generate the type of results we need. Leaders need alternatives that do. It is time to stop beating our people with carrots and sticks and embrace different, more effective leadership strategies.

When it comes to motivation, we have underestimated ourselves—and perhaps even cheated ourselves of something richer and much more meaningful than pellets, carrots, and sticks. By falling prey to the Pecking Pigeon Paradigm, we convinced ourselves that this was the nature of motivation, and we bypassed the more human reasons we work.

The new science of motivation is full of promise. There are alternatives to the Pecking Pigeon Paradigm and the constant grind to provide more and better pellets to get people to do what you want them to do. It shouldn't surprise you that people don't find those pigeon pellets satisfying.

This book is for leaders with the strength to question traditional beliefs and common practices. It is for leaders who recognize that outdated approaches to motivation compromise people's energy, creativity, well-being, and health—both mental and physical. This book is for leaders who want to cultivate a workplace where people flourish.

This book is for you if you yearn for a practical yet honorable way to achieve and sustain results that also brings out the best in—and for—people.

The Motivation Dilemma

Larry Lucchino found himself in an envious position. He had the perfect person in mind to recruit and hire as a new employee at the highest salary ever paid to someone in the role. He was authorized to include whatever it might take to motivate this person to work in his organization—signing bonus, moving allowance, transportation, housing, performance bonuses, and a high-status office.

Lucchino's mission: lure Billy Beane, the general manager of the small-market Oakland A's, to the Boston Red Sox, one of the most storied and prestigious franchises in baseball. Lucchino was impressed with Billy's innovative ideas about using SABRmetrics—a new statistical analysis for recruiting and developing players.

In 2002, the Red Sox offered Billy what was at the time the highest salary for a GM in baseball's history. The team enticed him with private jets and other extravagant perks. As you may know from Michael Lewis's book *Moneyball: The Art of Winning an Unfair Game* or from the hit movie starring Brad Pitt, Billy turned down the historic offer.

Billy's mom, Maril Adrian, one of my dearest friends, shared her perspective with me in real time as Billy's life unfolded in the media over the decade. She told me that Billy's values inspired his choices—especially his dedication to family and love of baseball.

Sports Illustrated corroborated her assertion: "After high school, Beane signed with the New York Mets based solely on money and later regretted it. That played into his decision this time."[1]

Every day, managers make the same mistake Lucchino made: they believe they can motivate people. It's not all the managers' fault. Armed with antiquated ideas about motivation, most organizations hold managers accountable for motivating people.

The motivation dilemma is that you are being held accountable for something you cannot do: motivate people.

Attempting to motivate people is a losing proposition, no matter your resources. Why? Because people are already motivated—but maybe not in the way you want. When you assume people aren't motivated, you tend to fall back to strategies proven ineffective, wrongheaded, or even counter to what you intended. You incentivize, and when that doesn't work, you add more carrots (rewards, incentives, bribes). When you run out of carrots, you may try wielding a thicker stick (threats, fearmongering, and punishment). At some point, you realize your attempts to motivate people are fruitless or, even worse, more harmful than beneficial.

The motivation dilemma begins with an erroneous premise—assuming people aren't motivated and the leader's job is to motivate them. I was sharing this idea with a group of managers in China when a man yelled, "Shocking! This is shocking!" Startled, we all jumped. It was highly unusual for a participant to yell out loud in a typically reserved audience. I asked him, "Why is this so shocking?" He replied, "My whole career, I have been told my job as a manager is to motivate my people. I have been held accountable for motivating my people. Now you tell me I cannot do it." "That's right," I told him. "So how does that make you feel?" "Shocked!" he repeated before adding, "And relieved."

I have witnessed an epiphany among managers and human resource professionals as they realize that depending on carrots and sticks is a flawed strategy to get people to pursue goals, adopt new habits, or change behavior. They recognize that they've been relying on old-fashioned methods without the benefit of empirical science that proves these strategies undermine the type of motivation needed for people to achieve results while simultaneously experiencing well-being.

Let go of the notion that you can and should motivate people.

Letting go of traditional approaches to motivation used to be challenging because we didn't understand the true nature of human motivation and the alternatives for tapping into people's natural vitality. Now we do.

Model That Reflects Reality: The Spectrum of Motivation

Traditional motivation approaches ask *if* people are motivated or not. But that's the wrong question. The question isn't even *what* motivates people. Lucchino and the Red Sox suspected Billy wasn't inclined to take a new job or move to the East Coast. They depended on traditional means to try to motivate—or manipulate—him. They might have discovered why he rejected their offer if they had understood that Billy was already motivated. They could have uncovered the *reasons* guiding Billy's choices.

People are always motivated. The crucial question is *why*.

**People are always motivated.
The crucial question is *why*.**

I'm willing to bet that when facilitating a team meeting, you know it's a mistake to assume that participants are motivated to be there just because they show up. But it's also a mistake to think they are unmotivated if they check their phones during the meeting. A more accurate and valuable conclusion is that everyone attending is motivated but not for the same reasons. Asking why people are motivated to be at your meeting leads to a spectrum of motivation possibilities represented as six motivational outlooks in the Spectrum of Motivation model, figure 1.1.[2]

The model reflects the reasons people do what they do. The six motivational outlooks describe six types of motivation or different reasons people might take action (or not). If we use the meeting as an example, notice how people can exhibit the same behavior (participate in the meeting) for different reasons that affect the quality of their energy:

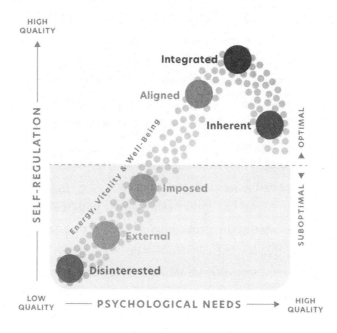

FIGURE 1.1 Spectrum of Motivation model—
six motivational outlooks

- *Disinterested motivational outlook*—They show up and go through the motions, even though they cannot find any value in the meeting; it feels like a waste of time, or they are so busy that attending adds to their sense of feeling overwhelmed.
- *External motivational outlook*—The meeting is an opportunity to demonstrate their power or status, which could also lead to more money or promotion in the future; attending is a chance to earn badges, kudos, or even a bonus or financial perk.
- *Imposed motivational outlook*—They feel pressure to attend because everyone else is attending, they fear what

might happen if they don't show up, or they hope their attendance will help them avoid feeling guilt, shame, or a sense that they've disappointed you.

- *Aligned motivational outlook*—They attend because they believe the meeting aligns with a significant personal value, such as learning; they feel attending is the right thing to do.
- *Integrated motivational outlook*—They link the meeting to their life or work purpose, such as giving voice to a meaningful issue; they self-identify with the reason for the meeting in a meaningful way ("I'm a sales leader, and this is what sales leaders do").
- *Inherent motivational outlook*—They simply enjoy meetings and thought it would be fun.

The outlooks are not on a continuum. Someone might experience one outlook when the meeting appears on their calendar, another as they walk into the room, and another depending on the discussed topic. Different motivational outlooks can pop up anytime, hence the model's bubbles.

Recognizing the six motivational outlooks is essential to effective leadership, but you must also appreciate why the Spectrum of Motivation has two halves.

The distinction between suboptimal and optimal motivation captures the chasm between traditional thinking and the new science of motivation:

- Three outlooks—disinterested, external, and imposed— are considered suboptimal. Outdated motivational theories revolve around suboptimal outlooks that reflect low-quality motivation. These outlooks represent motivational junk food that fails to generate positive energy, vitality, and a sense of well-being.

- Three outlooks—aligned, integrated, and inherent—are considered optimal. The new motivation science revolves around optimal outlooks that reflect high-quality motivation. Optimal outlooks represent motivational health food that generates the positive energy, vitality, and sense of well-being required to sustain the pursuit and achievement of meaningful goals while thriving and flourishing.

Appreciating how suboptimal and optimal motivational outlooks affect people's well-being, short-term productivity, and long-term performance is essential to leading at a higher level.

> The distinction between suboptimal and optimal motivation captures the chasm between traditional thinking and the new science of motivation.

The Downside of Motivational Junk Food

Consider this scenario. You buy dinner at a local drive-through—burgers, fries, and shakes—planning to eat at home with your family. But the aroma of those fries is intoxicating. You simply cannot help yourself—you eat one. By the time you arrive home, the bag of french fries is empty.

How do you feel after downing the package of french fries? Guilty or remorseful? Consider the effect junk food has on your mental energy. What happens to your physical energy even if you feel grateful and satisfied? It spikes dramatically and falls just as dramatically. How nourished is your body? A steady diet of junk food simply isn't good for you. Even if you can justify an occasional splurge, you are wise to understand your choices.

Suboptimal motivation is the equivalent of motivational junk food. When you entice people by promising more money, awarding prizes, offering rewards and badges, threatening punishment, applying pressure, and imposing guilt, shame, or emotional blackmail, you're offering them a motivational junk-food buffet. Using suboptimal motivational tactics to encourage specific behaviors from people has the same short- and long-term effects on their psychological health as junk food has on their physical health. Unfortunately, people find these rewards and punishments (carrots and sticks) as hard to resist as french fries.

Here's a too-common scenario. Your HR department sends employees an invitation to enter an incentive program. If they lose enough weight, they win an iPad. They think, "What do I have to lose except some weight? What do I have to gain except health and an iPad?" They should think again.

Researchers followed people who entered an organization-sponsored contest awarding prizes for losing weight.[3] They found that many people lost weight and won rewards. However, the studies were conducted only during the contest period. They didn't track maintenance. The research that incentive companies use to sell their extrinsic reward programs to organizations ends here, concluding that such programs are effective for helping people lose weight. The rest of the story is one that too many leaders and HR professionals have not heard.

If people participate, without perceived pressure, in a behavior-change program offering small financial incentives, they may be likely to change their behavior initially. But when researchers continue following the prizewinners after an incentive program ends, their findings mirror what extensive motivational research has proven about incentives: twelve weeks after winning their prize, people resume old behaviors, regain their lost weight, and add even more weight.[4]

Study after study verifies that tangible incentives do not sustain changes in personal health behaviors but undermine those behaviors over time. A heavy dose of motivational junk food might help people initiate new and healthy behaviors but fails miserably in assisting people to maintain their progress or sustain results. What may be more disturbing is that people are so discouraged, disillusioned, and debilitated by their failure that they are less likely to engage in further weight-loss attempts. If they do, they might game the system by going through the motions to get their reward but not expecting lasting change.

These extrinsically based schemes cost more than people realize: the participants' failure in one area of their life can affect their sense of efficacy in other areas. So why do over 70 percent of wellness programs in the United States use financial incentives and rewards programs to encourage healthy behavior changes?[5] The reasons below can apply to any incentive-based motivation scheme:

- Financial incentives, rewards, badges, and tokens are easy (if expensive) to offer.
- Organizations have not taken the time to create more innovative, healthy, and sustainable options.
- People feel entitled to receive incentives, and organizations are afraid to take them away.
- Leaders promote junk-food motivation to entice people to achieve goals or adopt certain behaviors because they simply don't question standard practices.
- Leaders have not learned how to facilitate people's shift to a more optimal and sustainable motivational outlook.
- People don't understand the nature of their motivation, so when they are unhappy at work, they ask for more money. They yearn for something different—but they don't know what it is—so they ask for the most apparent incentive: money or perks. Managers assume that their hands are tied because they can't comply with someone's request for more money.[6]

The Upside of Motivational Health Food

Kacey is perennially a top salesperson in her organization. She felt offended when her company announced a contest to award top sellers with a weeklong spa trip. "Do they think I do what I do so I can win a week at a spa? Maybe it sounds corny, but I work hard because I love what I do. I get great satisfaction from solving my clients' problems and seeing the difference it makes. If my company wants to connect with me and show appreciation, that's different. That isn't the case. If they knew me, they would understand that as a single mother, a spa week away is not a reward but an imposition."

People with high-quality motivation, such as Kacey, may accept external rewards when offered, but this is not the reason for their efforts. The reasons the Kaceys of the world do what they do are more profound and provide more satisfaction than external rewards can deliver.

Kacey would have found it easier if her organization had been more attuned to her needs rather than falling into the junk-food belief that salespeople are motivated by money and rewards. Instead, she found herself in an awkward situation. Kacey didn't want to get sucked into the low-quality motivation of the reward trip. Still, she feared offending her manager and colleagues by refusing the trip or complaining about the options.

Being an exemplary self leader, Kacey initiated a meeting with her manager to discuss the situation. She explained how the incentive program had the opposite effect than her manager had probably intended. She declared that she would continue selling and servicing her customers with her usual high standards—regardless of winning a reward. Kacey and her manager both described the conversation as "liberating." They felt it deepened their relationship because the manager now understood Kacey's internal dedication to her work.

At the end of the next sales cycle, Kacey exceeded her goals based on her own high-quality reasons. Instead of imposing a reward on her, Kacey's manager conferred with her about how he could express his gratitude for her achievements within fair price and time boundaries. Kacey chose an activity that she and her young child could enjoy together. Rather than interpreting the reward trip as a carrot to work harder, Kacey interpreted it as an expression of her organization's gratitude. She reported how different the experience was from previous award trips: "The week took on special significance as a heartfelt thank-you from my manager and a wonderful memory-making experience with my child."

Kacey's deepened relationship with her manager and feeling valued were far more rewarding than winning a contest. When people experience high-quality motivation, the implications for the organization are significant. They achieve above-standard results; demonstrate enhanced creativity, collaboration, and productivity; are more likely to repeat their peak performance; and enjoy increased physical and mental health.[7]

Junk Food or Health Food—You Choose

The three suboptimal motivational outlooks—disinterested, external, and imposed—are the junk foods of motivation. Their tangible or intangible rewards can be enticing at the moment but do not lead to flourishing—far from it. People with a suboptimal motivational outlook are less likely to have the energy it takes to achieve their goals. But even if they do, they are less likely to experience the positive energy, vitality, or sense of well-being required to sustain their performance over time.[8]

The three optimal motivational outlooks—aligned, integrated, and inherent—are the health foods of motivation. They may require more thought and preparation, but they generate the high-quality energy, vitality, and positive well-being that lead to sustainable results.

Case in Point: Himesh and the Lab Tech

On his first day back at a plant in India, after a training session on the Spectrum of Motivation, Himesh encountered one of his employees with low-quality motivation.[9]

Himesh noticed his technical service executive discussing something with an external contractor in the lab. Himesh saw that the technician was wearing safety glasses, but she had not followed plant procedures to ensure the contractor was also protected.

Himesh is a strict manager with a no-tolerance policy regarding breaking safety regulations. His typical response to this flagrant breach of policy would be to call the technician to his office and, in his words, "read her the riot act." By the way, this is why Himesh had been in the training class. His plant's engagement scores were among the lowest in a global company with more than fifty thousand employees.

According to Himesh's self-assessment, "I am known to blow a fuse (or two) when people flout safety rules. However, I managed to keep my cool and decided to test my training." He asked the technician to come to his office. He could see that she was worried about his reaction. Instead of leading with his dismay and disappointment, Himesh started by explaining that he had just received some training on motivation. He shared core concepts with her. He then asked her if she thought the rule to wear safety glasses when no experiment was happening was stupid, as there is no danger to the eyes. Did she feel imposed upon by having to wear safety glasses at all times?

Since Himesh had invited the technician to have a discussion rather than a dressing down, she was open and candid.

She explained that she had a two-year-old child and was highly concerned about lab safety, as she wanted to reach home safe every evening. To Himesh's surprise, she also shared that she would prefer even more stringent safety measures in certain areas. For example, she suggested they require safety shoes for lab experiments conducted at elevated temperatures. But she could not understand the rationale for wearing safety glasses when no one was conducting experiments. Indeed, the technician expressed her resentment about the imposed rule. She didn't feel compelled to enforce it, especially with an external contractor.

Himesh listened and genuinely acknowledged her feelings. He then provided his rationale behind the regulation, explaining his hope and intention that wearing glasses would become a habit that protects people's lives, just like wearing a safety belt in the car.

Himesh said, "I saw the light dawn in her eyes."

It is important to note that Himesh did not attempt to motivate the technician. He recognized that she was already motivated. She was motivated not to follow the regulation. He challenged his natural tendency to rush to judgment and took the time to explore why she was motivated the way she was. By understanding the nature of her motivation, he had more options on how to lead.

He reported: "I am sure if I had followed my normal instincts and given her a piece of my mind, I would have been met with a hangdog look, profuse apologies, and a promise to never do this again. And it probably would have happened again. She would have gone away from my office with feelings of resentment and being imposed upon, and I would also have had a disturbed day due to all the negative energy."

Himesh's approach helped his technician shift her motivation from low quality (imposed outlook) to higher quality (aligned outlook). As he reported, "Suffice it to say that in my view, my little experiment was a success. I have shared what I learned with many of my team members and I plan to have more motivational outlook conversations with them in the coming weeks."

Recapping "The Motivation Dilemma"

The motivation dilemma is that even though motivating people doesn't work, leaders are held accountable for doing it. This dilemma has led to ineffective motivational leadership practices. Traditional motivational tactics focus on obtaining short-term results. Pushing for results, you discover that pressure, tension, and external drives prevent people from attaining those results. Even short-term gains can't compare to the loss of creativity, innovation, physical health, and mental well-being. Adding insult to injury, suboptimal motivation all but destroys long-term prospects.

Motivating people does not work because they are already motivated—they are always motivated in one of the six ways reflected in the Spectrum of Motivation. So if motivating people doesn't work, what does? The next chapter reveals alternatives to motivational junk food and the healthy options that could be the answer to your motivation dilemma.

What Motivates People: The Real Story

Why do you get out of bed in the morning—and stay up?

What does it take to walk away from the five-hundred-calorie muffin instead of caving in to the temptation?

How does your angry, defensive, or self-righteous energy differ from your loving, compassionate, and joyful energy?

Answers to these compelling questions come from motivation science: humans have an innate tendency and desire to thrive. People want to grow, develop, and be fully functioning. Of course, science is just catching up to what creative and thoughtful people have understood throughout our existence. Ancient and modern artists and musicians continue to capture our yearning for self-identity, growth, and a meaningful connection to others. Poets such as Kahlil Gibran, Maya Angelou, and Robert Frost have reflected our longing for wholeness. Movies such as *The Wizard of Oz*, *Star Wars*, and *Gravity* portray our nature to thrive. We want to flourish—but we cannot do it alone. We are, by nature, social animals. Striving to reach our human potential is natural, yet we innately recognize that the interconnection between ourselves and the world around us is vital to that process.

Our desire to thrive may be innate, but thriving doesn't happen automatically—especially at work. Just because we gravitate toward psychological growth and integration doesn't guarantee it will happen. Human thriving in the workplace is a dynamic potential that requires nurturing. The workplace facilitates, fosters, and enables our flourishing, or it disrupts, thwarts, and impedes it. Conventional motivational practices have often undermined human potential more than encouraged it.

> **Human thriving in the workplace is a dynamic potential that requires nurturing.**

The bad news is that we have paid a high price for working with outdated ideas about motivation. The good news is that the science of motivation can emerge as both a radical departure and an exciting opportunity.

If you learn the real story of motivation, you will experience a shift in how you live and work—and, importantly, in how you lead.

Illuminating the True Nature of Human Motivation

The title of this book states that motivating people does not work. It also promises an answer to the question, What does work? The essence of the answer lies at the heart of motivation science and the validation of three psychological needs—choice, connection, and competence. Regardless of gender, race, culture, or generation, the real story behind motivation is as simple and complex as whether your psychological needs are fulfilled.

For confirmation that these three psychological needs are essential to human thriving and flourishing, you can delve into the plentiful evidence provided by research over the past sixty years (much of it referenced throughout this book and listed in the notes, references, and resources sections). You can consider the anecdotal evidence in the stories, examples, and case studies generated from my experience applying these ideas in more than forty countries over the past twenty years. Or you can also simply observe babies and toddlers. As you will discover in the following three sections of this chapter, our psychological needs for choice, connection, and competence play out from the moment we are born.

The First Psychological Need: Choice (Autonomy)

Our need to perceive we have a choice, a sense of control, and autonomy—and the effects of *not* having them—has been at the forefront of motivation research since the early 1960s.[1]

Choice is our human need to perceive we have choices, feel we have options within boundaries, and have a sense of control that we are the source of our actions.

An excellent example of choice is what happens when you feed a baby. What does the baby do as you bring a spoonful of food to his mouth? He grabs for the spoon—he wants to do it himself. He wants to be the source of that food going into his mouth. Despite not having the skill to feed himself, he needs to control the situation. If a high chair restrains him, he will shut his mouth or turn his head, which explains the orange smear of mashed carrots across babies' faces in most mealtime photos.

You may remember the animated Maypo cereal commercials if you are a certain age. If not, you can watch these classics on YouTube. In one of my favorites, a father tries to get his child to eat the maple-flavored oat cereal. The kid will have none of it. The father plays games with the spoon, hoping to entice his child to eat his Maypo, but as soon as the spoon comes near the kid's mouth, he clamps his mouth shut. Finally, the father appeals to the little boy's love of cowboys and pretends to be a cowboy taking a bite of the cereal. After one bite, the father realizes he loves the cereal and starts chowing it down himself. The kid sees his dad enjoying and eating all his cereal and cries out, "I want my Maypo!" Any parent engaged in reverse psychology appeals to a child's need for autonomy. (Beware, however, that those tactics are likely to backfire. Children can detect manipulation a mile away. If they feel you are manipulating them, you are undermining their second psychological need, for connection.)

Over the past twenty years, various studies indicate that adults never lose their psychological need for choice.[2] For example, productivity increases significantly for blue-collar workers in manufacturing plants when they can stop the line. So does the productivity of white-collar workers in major investment banking firms who report a high sense of autonomy. Employees experience autonomy when they feel some control and choice about the work they do. Choice doesn't mean managers are permissive or hands-off but that people believe they can influence the workplace. You may consider "empowerment" a cliché, but if people don't have a sense of empowerment, their sense of choice suffers, as well as their productivity and performance.[3]

Some find it challenging to grasp that everything they do is their own choice—that they choose their level of autonomy. That's why so many people feel constrained at work. Yet a workplace axiom says that autonomy is 20 percent given and 80 percent taken. Whether formally empowered or not, people have a choice to get out of bed, go to work, accept goals, and make a contribution—or not. Anytime they take the position of not having options, they undermine their experience of choice. Having said that, some leaders make it tougher for people to interpret the workplace as being full of choices.

I was curious about an article with this provocative title: "If You Want to Motivate Someone, Shut Up Already."[4] To find out more, I called Dr. Brandon Irwin, the lead researcher cited in the article, who shared some motivational practices that don't work the way we thought. Brandon explained that, initially, his team was surprised to learn that when a sports or training coach is vocal and verbally encouraging a trainee, performance is significantly lower than the results achieved with a quiet but attentive coach.[5]

Brandon hypothesizes that in light of what we know about the need for choice, quiet coaches get better results than verbal ones because verbal encouragement externalizes the exercisers' attention and energy. When coaches encourage their trainee to "do one more; come on, you can do it; keep up the energy," the motivation shifts from internal to external—blocking the exercisers' sense of choice. The external encouragement and praising subverted the trainees' inner desire to perform, push, and excel, thus limiting their capacity to do so.

Brandon and his team tried incentives to offset the distraction of the verbally encouraging coach. If exercisers achieved a challenging goal (despite the verbal coaching), they would receive a prize, such as a free gym membership. Their results were consistent with studies showing how rewards tend to diminish performance in the short and long term. The added distraction of an external incentive—more motivational junk food—further blocked the exercisers' perception of choice, impaired their ability to tap into their internal resources, and lowered performance even more.[6]

As a leader, you can benefit from Brandon's discovery about vocal sports coaches and the impact leadership has on people's ability to experience choice. You'll discover that his research also has implications for the second psychological need—connection.

The Second Psychological Need: Connection (Relatedness)

What does a toddler do when she is talking to you, and you aren't looking at her? She grabs your face in her tiny hands and turns it in her direction, forcing you to look her in the eyes. Even in societies where someone of lesser status looking someone of a higher rank in the eye is not appropriate, children do it anyway; their natural response is to connect. No matter our age, social station, or culture, connection is one of our three psychological needs.

 Connection is our need to feel a sense of belonging and genuine connection to others without concerns about ulterior motives, to align goals and actions to meaningful values and a sense of purpose, and to contribute to something greater than ourselves.

Notice the range of needs that connection covers. It is personal, interpersonal, and social. We thrive on connection.[7]

Several years ago, a worldwide electronics giant hired me to deliver a keynote to its top global leaders in London. My speech was the last event standing between these one hundred leaders and their trip home after a weeklong conference. As I was about to go on stage, my host gave me a heads-up. She explained that they were spent and might be restless during my ninety-minute speech. My host also apologized for their multitasking culture. She told me that speakers had complained all week about the lack of attention and the constant texting and emailing.

My host's warnings sparked my competitive nature—I would show them! I would be so compelling that they would forget about going home, cease multitasking, and sit with rapt attention. About three minutes into my presentation, I was humbled. I did not have one person's eye contact. I could have been talking to a wall. I was talking to a wall—and it made me sad. Spontaneously, I decided to do something I had heard tales of from fellow speakers but, given my extroverted nature, had never dared to do. I shut up and just stood there—waiting, waiting—until the silence captured the audience's attention, and I had every eye in the room staring at me curiously.

After an eternity, I slowly and quietly asked, "What is going on here? For some reason, your organization thought it was worth thousands of dollars to fly me thousands of miles to talk to you about these ideas that might make a difference in how you lead. Obviously, you disagree. I'll make you a deal. Give me fifteen minutes. That is all I ask—fifteen minutes. If I cannot say something of value to you in fifteen minutes, I do not deserve your attention, and you can go back to your cell phones, tablets, and computers."

They were now staring in disbelief. I had them—except for one young man who promptly returned to his keyboard and in a loud voice exclaimed, "Well, I can multitask, can't I?" I moved as close to him as I could before responding, thoroughly tongue-in-cheek. "You could if you were a woman." The group broke out in laughter. I had chosen the right guy to pick on. He looked up, smiled, and said, "Okay, hit me with your best stuff."

But instead of throwing my "stuff" at them, I abandoned the speech I had planned and led the group in a heartfelt discussion about what had just happened. I shared how I felt trying to do a good job and convey the ideas I was passionate about without their attention or any visible signs of appreciation from them. They talked about their fear of letting go of their electronic devices and not being in constant contact with people. We explored how none of us had been getting our basic psychological need for connection satisfied. It turned into one of those magical moments where we all learned something.

One of their big aha moments was realizing how few of them—or the people they lead—were getting their connection needs met through work. Their employees' desire to be in constant contact with friends outside of work was due to their lack of connection at work—especially those in Gen X or millennial generations.[8]

I ask you to consider the question I asked that group of global leaders: What percentage of your waking hours are connected to your work? Considering the time it takes to get ready for work, get to work, get home from work, and decompress, you probably average 75 percent of your waking hours connected to your work. If your need for connection is not met at work, where is it met? As leading researcher Dr. Jacques Forest told me, need satisfaction is essential for everyone, all the time and everywhere. If you do not satisfy your needs for connection through your work, you will not likely compensate for it in the limited amount of time you have outside of work.[9]

We can all fall prey to attempting to substitute missing psychological needs. Collecting more Facebook friends and LinkedIn contacts, nabbing the big corner office, and winning the top prize in a competition are obvious examples. The phenomenon is called *compensatory need satisfaction*. And try as we might to find external fixes to an internal longing, it simply doesn't work.

Your role as a leader is to help people experience authentic connection at work so people can care about others and feel cared about, experience relationships devoid of ulterior motives, and contribute to the welfare of the greater good.

Remember the study by Dr. Brandon Irwin in the previous section describing the psychological need for choice? His research showed that silent coaches garnered higher productivity from exercisers than verbally encouraging coaches. It is important to note that having a coach at all mattered. People performed better with an exercise coach than without one. But you cannot deny the impact the type of coaching had. Brandon believes that connection also played a big part in the results.

The exercisers thought the verbal coaches were not acting in their best interest but were self-serving. In some cases, the exercisers interpreted verbal pushing as the coach's need to win. In other cases, if exercisers perceived that the coach's ability to perform the goals he gave them was inferior to their own ability, they interpreted the verbal encouragement as being more for the coach's own motivation than for the people he was coaching.

This finding is essential when it comes to interpersonal relationships at work. Your people will feel the opposite of connection if they think you or the organization is using them, believe your attention is not genuine, or suspect they are a means to someone else's ends.

You can't force someone to feel a sense of connection. But as a leader, you can encourage connection by challenging beliefs and practices that undermine people's connection at work. That means paying attention to how your people feel and gaining the skill to deal with their emotions. That means getting personal.

The Third Psychological Need: Competence

Do you ever delight in watching babies learn to walk? What do you notice? They fall—a lot. You never question why they fall because they are learning. But have you ever questioned why they get back up? Why are they smiling and giggling instead of crying when they pull themselves up to try again? The answer is that they find joy in learning, growing, and gaining mastery. Our third psychological need is competence.

 Competence is our need to feel effective at meeting everyday situations, demonstrate skill over time, and feel a sense of growth and flourishing.

Anyone around a two-year-old has experienced the toddler's constant question, "Why?" Why does the toddler ask why? Because she loves growing and learning. We encourage her learning by setting up systems, such as school. But then we begin spurring her on with sticks in the form of stress to earn good grades and pressure to be at the top of her class and urge her to engage in activities that look good on college applications. We evaluate her learning, rewarding her positive performance with carrots in the form of gold stars, public praise, and student-of-the-month awards. Have you ever considered what happens to the 99.9 percent of children who do not receive the rewards?

Some school systems started to see the futility of incentive programs to reward the few and discourage the many. Now the trend is "Everyone gets a trophy!" This solution does not provide the effective teaching or realistic feedback our children need to satisfy their competence.

Motivating children to learn won't work for the same reason that motivating adults doesn't work—they are already motivated to learn. Children have a psychological need to learn and grow. Bribing them with carrots or driving them with sticks diverts them from their natural love of learning. We question what happened to a child's sense of wonder as we watch him years later, just going through the motions at work. Children who succumbed to ineffective motivational techniques for learning and growing are now in the workplace, hooked on motivational junk food in the form of pay-for-performance plans and elaborate reward and incentive programs.

Motivating people doesn't work because you can't impose growth and learning on them. But you can promote a learning environment that doesn't undermine your people's sense of competence. What message do we send about the importance of competence when training is one of the first items cut in economically challenging times? What does it say about our belief in people's growth when educational opportunities focus on or are limited to managers and high-level executives?

Most organizations provide individual contributors with basic hard-skill training required to do the job. But investing in people's capacity to excel is less common. Organizations that invest in teaching people the soft skills required for psychological thriving—what I call *psychological sense*—are rarer.[10] That's too bad on two levels:

- People need to have a sense of competence in every area of their lives—especially where they spend most of their time. If they do not experience a sense of competence at work, there is a good chance they will not have a holistic experience of competence—which negatively affects every aspect of their lives.[11]
- The organization suffers by not training individual contributors in self leadership skills. Research indicates that the most essential ingredient in a successful company initiative is the proactive behavior of the individuals tasked with implementing the change. Some good news: proactive behavior can be taught and learned. Researchers recommend that allocating more resources to teaching these so-called soft skills to nonmanagers is a better investment of training budgets.[12]

You miss a great opportunity at the end of the day if you only ask, "What did you achieve today?" Try adding, "What did you learn today? How did you grow?"

Psychological Needs: The Building Blocks of Motivation

Notice the connection between psychological needs and motivational outlooks. As you can see in the Spectrum of Motivation model, figure 2.1, when people experience

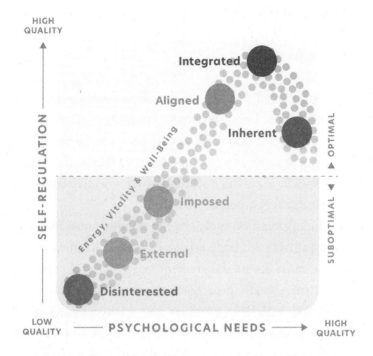

FIGURE 2.1 Spectrum of Motivation model—psychological needs

high-quality psychological needs, they have an optimal motivational outlook. (The color version of the Spectrum of Motivation model, as seen in the front of this book, reflects these three optimal motivational outlooks as high-frequency colors of the rainbow—blue, purple, and violet.) In other words, if their needs for choice, connection, and competence are satisfied, the result is an aligned, integrated, or inherent motivational outlook.

When people experience low-quality psychological needs, they'll end up with a suboptimal motivational outlook. (The color version of the Spectrum of Motivation model reflects these three suboptimal motivational outlooks as low-vibrating colors of the rainbow—red, orange, and green.) In other words, if their needs for choice, connection, and competence are not satisfied, the result is a disinterested, external, or imposed motivational outlook.

The Domino Effect

Even though I described each of the three psychological needs individually, appreciating the combined power of choice, connection, and competence is relevant to effective leadership.

Imagine you have a controlling manager. She micromanages people and projects—whether they need it or not. She either fails to acknowledge or doesn't care about the opportunity loss she creates through her inappropriate leadership style and its impact on the psychological needs of those she leads. She seems content with not changing her ways—after all, she has successfully moved up in the organization.

You have proven yourself to her over the years, especially when collecting sales data and submitting the quarterly report to headquarters. When she took a leave of absence, you completed the reports independently. Yet she still demands reviewing and editing your work and sending it to headquarters herself. The changes she makes seem arbitrary. There is simply no pleasing her. Her micromanagement is undermining your sense of choice—she is controlling your work and not allowing you to think for yourself. You are afraid to go over her head to complain because you've seen what happens to complainers.

The Domino Effect has begun. Your manager's control erodes your perception of choice but has you second-guessing your competence. Your inability to manage your manager's overinvolvement or the organizational politics further erodes your competence. Your manager's ineffective leadership, lack of sensitivity to your needs, and apparent self-interest prevent any sense of connection. External forces—her micromanaging style and your fear—dictate your internal sense of well-being.

When it comes to completing your reports, you do them because you are afraid of what will happen if you don't. You have an imposed motivational outlook. Driven by fear and maybe a little guilt, you do your job while thinking, "I will do the reports because I have to, but I resent it. I will do just enough to get by." You do not bother to think about the work creatively or add quality because your manager would probably change your work anyway.

Then, more bad news. You begin to generalize your suboptimal motivational outlook by thinking, "The only reason I get up every day is to collect my paycheck." Suddenly you have an external motivational outlook toward your whole job—it has become all about the money. You would leave if the economy was better and jobs were easier to find.

When all three psychological needs are satisfied, people thrive with positive energy, vitality, and a sense of well-being. But—and this is a big *but*—one need depends on the others. Eroding choice, connection, or competence diminishes the others as well. The Domino Effect begins when even one psychological need is missing.

Don't be the boss described in this section! People cite their micromanaging boss as one of the greatest threats to their optimal motivation at work.

Case in Point: The Art of Schmoozing

As the food and beverage director at a midsize resort, Art enjoyed immediate success with his approach: "For waiters, it's all about the tips." He explained, "I teach my waitstaff how to get better tips through schmoozing. They are motivated because the more they chat up customers, use their names, ooze charm, and even touch them appropriately, the higher their tips. They see a direct cause and effect."

His approach was working. Most of the waitstaff were generating more tips. We need to consider what motivational outlook Art's tactics encouraged. His focus on increased tips gave his waitstaff a sense of choice: "If I choose to schmooze, I'll get more tips." Art's focus on specific behaviors and the immediate feedback of higher tips reinforced their success, growth, learning, and probably a sense of competence.

Art didn't see the Domino Effect coming. While Art's approach seemed to satisfy his people's need for choice and competence, he was ignoring connection. Art undervalued the relationship between a waitstaff and the people they served in a people-oriented business. Beyond earning more tips, few of his waitstaff had a sense of meaning or deeper purpose to their work.

At the end of the night, a typical comment from a waiter reflected an external motivational outlook: "Wow, look at all the tips I made!" Consider the qualitative difference between that comment and one reflecting an optimal motivational outlook: "I think I may have been the only good thing that happened to that couple tonight. They came in grumpy but left laughing. It felt good to run interference for Tony when he got behind on two of his tables. We were cranking as a team tonight—like a well-oiled machine. I had fun! I made a difference. And wow, on top of all that, I made money doing something I enjoy, am good at, and find meaningful."

Art missed the opportunity to create a workplace where his staff could experience the power of optimal motivation. He could have teed up success as building relationships, improving service, or establishing repeat customers rather than earning more tips. He could have helped his staff tap into their values for service, creativity in making improvements, or enjoyment of their job. He could have shown them how satisfaction comes from making a positive difference in a person's dining experience or their own sense of joy in their work. Art could have fostered a more profound experience for his staff by helping them shift from an external motivational outlook.

Not understanding the real story of motivation returned to haunt him. Art's focus on external motivation was not sustainable. When his staff had mastered schmoozing and maximized their tips, they had no other areas to grow in. When the season slowed down, the economy slumped, and staff couldn't schmooze more tips out of people, their performance also slowed and slumped.

When his staff and the customers they served started to complain, turnover increased. Art's response was "The only way I can get people to improve their performance is to pay them more, set up recognition programs, and reward and incentivize them to work harder. And I don't have the budget for that."

Art did what most organizations do when they don't have enough money to keep elevating pay and incentives to

motivate people using traditional approaches to motivation—
he pegged the role of the waiter as a high-turnover job. He tried
to justify hiring and training costs as expected in the industry.
He blamed incompetent people for the negative impact on
sales and customer devotion.

Imagine if Art understood the psychological needs foundational to people's optimal motivation. He could have helped
his staff generate the vitality required to sustain high performance no matter the season. He could have encouraged choice,
connection, and competence by providing more options for
succeeding, helping the staff discover the meaning and value
of serving others, and encouraging creativity and new skills.

The irony was that the resort owners came to see Art as
incompetent and let him go. They decided that the food and
beverage director is a high-turnover position.

Recapping "What Motivates People: The Real Story"

What you misinterpret as someone's lack of motivation is
probably suboptimal motivation. The Spectrum of Motivation
reflects suboptimal motivation as a disinterested, external, or
imposed motivational outlook. When people experience optimal motivation, they enjoy vitality and a sense of well-being
reflected in the Spectrum of Motivation as an aligned, integrated, or inherent motivational outlook.

People's desire for something more in the workplace is
often mistaken as wanting more money, power, and status—
the external motivational outlook. Or they might yearn for a
release from feelings of fear, anger, pressure, imposition, and

pain—the imposed motivational outlook. But people are learners who long to grow, enjoy their work, be productive, sustain high performance, achieve goals, make positive contributions, and build lasting relationships—not because of motivational forces outside themselves but because it is human nature.

The real story of motivation is that many people suffer from suboptimal motivation without realizing the source of their longing is to fulfill the psychological needs fundamental to their well-being and thriving: choice, connection, and competence.

> The real story of motivation is that many people suffer from suboptimal motivation without realizing the source of their longing is to fulfill the psychological needs fundamental to their well-being and thriving: choice, connection, and competence.

3

Shifting Out of Overdrive

Drive results. Drive growth. Drive employee engagement. Drive behaviors.

Have you noticed how often the word *drive* is used in business conversations? A quick internet search reveals an exponential spike over the past few years in websites that refer to driving something besides cars and computers. Do yourself and the people you lead a favor. Recognize the danger of overdrive. You can drive cattle or a golf ball. But driving people for results, performance, or motivation only drives them crazy.

> You can drive cattle or a golf ball. But driving people for results, performance, or motivation only drives them crazy.

The road to driving everything from results to people's motivation was paved by Drive Theory, one of the most popular motivational theories of the past one hundred years. Influenced by burgeoning biological studies, researchers reasoned that people are motivated—or driven—by an instinctive need to get what they don't have. For example, an unsatisfied biological need generates a psychological tension that drives us to seek physiological balance or homeostasis. The theory is based on the big three biological needs: food, water, and sex. If you are hungry, you are driven to eat; if you are thirsty, you are driven to drink. (Perhaps this is the genesis of the age-old axiom to eat, drink, and be merry.)

Drive Theory makes sense for biological needs. Cell deprivation and unmet biological needs lead to a psychological drive to attain physiological balance. But as a general theory of motivation, it misses the mark. Drives dissipate when they are satiated (such as thirst when we drink water or hunger when we eat). When your biological needs are satiated, you are not driven to act until your body is deficient again. The problem is Drive Theory can't explain why people are motivated to eat when they're not hungry or to drink when they aren't thirsty. It doesn't explain why we do what we do beyond our desire to satiate biological needs. But the motivation theory based on psychological needs does.

Anti-Drive Theory

People's motivation—or energy to act—depends on their psychological needs for choice, connection, and competence. When psychological needs are satisfied, people experience optimal motivation. When those needs are thwarted, they experience suboptimal motivation. The idea that motivation stems from psychological needs—not drives—is an important distinction. Psychological needs are the opposite of Drive Theory's biological needs and psychological drives. When people's psychological needs are satisfied, their motivation is not diminished. Instead, the positive energy, vitality, and sense of well-being they experience leave them wanting more. You have probably experienced this with your own positive addictions, such as running, meditating, volunteering, playing with children, or being in the flow during an activity you enjoy.

When it comes to thriving, satisfying people's psychological needs for choice, connection, and competence is as important as satiating their biological needs for food, water, and sex.

> **When it comes to thriving, satisfying people's psychological needs for choice, connection, and competence is as important as satiating their biological needs for food, water, and sex.**

Being Driven Is Motivational Junk Food

Brandt, an executive in a prestigious electronics company, described himself to me as "intensely driven." With his permission, I questioned, "Why do you say you are driven? By what? Who is doing the driving? Are you driven by the promise of money, rewards, power, or status? Are you driven to dispel fear,

shame, or guilt? Are you driven to avoid disappointing someone important or yourself?"

Brandt admitted he was longing for something he couldn't
define. He felt out of balance physically, mentally, and emotionally. Together we explored several potential factors:

- Underlying reasons for his intense work behavior, which
  was affecting the quality of his family life
- Gaps between values he espoused versus the values he
  was living, which were affecting his health
- Differences between his dreams and his reality, which
  was unfulfilling and a disappointment

Brandt acknowledged that external factors were driving
him and prompting his emotions, feelings, and actions. Those
factors, it turned out, stemmed from his need to prove himself,
fueled by a desire to impress his father—who happened to be
a legend in the computer industry.

It didn't take long for Brandt to discover that "being driven"
is another way of saying, "I am not in control."

Discovering that unexplored emotions and beliefs are at
the root of dysfunctional behavior is not a revolutionary idea.
But the motivation science explaining why they are at the root
of dysfunctional behavior is groundbreaking. Dysfunctional
behavior is a response to our psychological needs for choice,
connection, and competence being thwarted, eroded, or
undermined. When these three psychological needs are satisfied, we experience a sense of control, meaning, and the ability
to cope with what life throws at us.

Brandt had been driven by motivational junk food for years—a craving for praise, validation, and tangible rewards and a fear of letting his father down. His drive to live up to self-imposed standards measured through promotions, financial success, and public recognition robbed him of his sense of choice. Ironically, his desire to please his father prevented him from experiencing a true and authentic sense of connection. Brandt's competence always felt diminished in comparison to his perception of his father's competence. Brandt was highly driven but to all the wrong places for the wrong reasons.

Two years after the conversation with Brandt, I met him at a business lunch. I didn't recognize him! He had lost weight and literally transformed his physical appearance. I asked, "What happened?" He told me he had grasped the danger of drive and focused instead on experiencing choice, connection, and competence. He smiled broadly as he explained, "For years I was trying to survive on junk-food motivation. I was eating way too many french fries—literally and psychologically."

People who experience choice, connection, and competence are thriving. They do not need something or someone else doing the driving.

Optimal Motivation Is Fragile

People want to thrive. People thrive when they experience the optimal motivation generated by satisfying choice, connection, and competence. What's the problem then?

Optimal motivation is fragile.[1] The combined potency of choice, connection, and competence is diminished if one of them is lacking. Driving performance, results, and behaviors can easily distract people from experiencing at least one of their psychological needs in various ways:

- Applying pressure to perform, win contests, or gain power and status can obscure people's sense of *choice*.
- Tempting people with junk-food motivation in the form of incentives, rewards, and external recognition can distract people from more meaningful motivation and destroy people's sense of *connection*.
- Driving change without giving people the training and resources to cope effectively threatens their sense of *competence*.

Your leadership can protect people's psychological needs from all these distractions. But first, you need to acknowledge the significance of the vertical axis on the Spectrum of Motivation model labeled *self-regulation*.

The Nature of Self-Regulation

Self-regulation is mindfully managing feelings, thoughts, values, and purpose for immediate and sustained positive effort.[2]

Your leadership either promotes or thwarts people's high-quality self-regulation. Notice the vertical axis on the Spectrum of Motivation model, figure 3.1. When you drive people's behavior—enticing or pressuring them with motivation junk food—you're probably pushing them into low-quality self-regulation and suboptimal motivation. Understanding the nature of self-regulation will help you create a workplace where

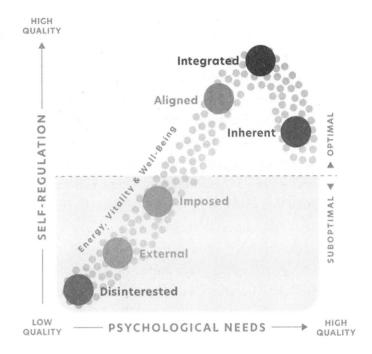

FIGURE 3.1 Spectrum of Motivation model—self-regulation

people are more likely to experience optimal motivation with high-quality self-regulation.[3]

Eating the Marshmallow

Put a marshmallow in front of a kid and ask him to wait for fifteen minutes before eating it. Then leave the room and watch what happens via hidden cameras. That's what researchers did at Stanford University in the late 1960s and early 1970s: they told children if they waited fifteen minutes to eat their one marshmallow, they would receive an additional one.[4] In the research footage, you can see the children's eyes light up at the prospect of two marshmallows! The purpose of the experiment was to measure the children's capacity for delayed gratification. What follows next is eye-opening—and hilarious.

Some children lasted mere seconds before popping the marshmallow in their mouths. Others tried to wait. The techniques kids used to keep themselves from eating the marshmallow were fascinating. They covered their eyes, pretended to sleep, and walked around the room. Some kids licked the marshmallow to a puddle but refused to chew it. Some kids sniffed it until they almost inhaled it.

Years later, researchers revisited the subjects and compared their delayed-gratification scores to current life measures, including SAT scores, level of education, and body mass index. They found a striking correlation. The children who had been able to delay their gratification for the marshmallow the longest—those with the greatest degree of self-regulation— had higher life-measure scores. Researchers postulated that children with a higher quality of self-regulation had a greater likelihood of later-life success.

The marshmallow studies made a great case for self-regulation as a crucial element of later success. However, as an advocate for self leadership, I had concerns that some might interpret the results to mean that self-regulation is something people are born with rather than something they choose or can develop. This is why research by the University of Rochester in 2012 captured my attention.[5] These researchers wondered what effect children's rational thought processes played in their capacity to self-regulate. In the Rochester experiments, "teachers" set up an art project to explore why some children demonstrate higher-quality self-regulation than others.

Children were put into one of two scenarios—a reliable situation and an unreliable situation. The children were told they had a choice: they could start their art project immediately with the materials at hand (a few old, used crayons in a glass jar) or they could wait for the teacher to get the big supply of art materials. All the children elected to wait for the good stuff. A moment later the teacher in the reliable situation returned with the big supply as promised; in the unreliable situation, she returned with an apology for not having the big supply after all.

In the videos of the experiments, the first thing you notice is the children's reactions when the supplies arrive and the profound disappointment when they don't. The letdown of not getting bigger and better supplies as promised made them less likely to engage enthusiastically in their art.

Although this development was interesting, with implications that go beyond children and art projects and into the workplace, the Rochester researchers weren't studying this aspect. They were still concerned about those marshmallows. As the children continued their art projects with hidden cameras still on, the teacher announced it was time for a snack. The children were given another choice: eat a marshmallow now or wait for the teacher to come back with two marshmallows.

Viewing the videos, you can witness many of the same tactics used by kids in the original marshmallow studies. Again, the kids' eyes light up at the prospect of two marshmallows. One kid nibbles the bottom of the marshmallow and puts it back on the plate, hoping no one will notice. One little boy sits on the marshmallow—out of sight, out of mind? Eventually, all the children eat their marshmallow within fifteen minutes.

There was one telling difference in these marshmallow studies compared to the original. Children in the reliable group, those who had received their nicer art supplies as promised, had delayed gratification times four times longer (twelve minutes on average) than the children who experienced the unreliable situation (three minutes on average). The quality of the children's self-regulation significantly correlated to their environment and experience.

Researchers concluded that when children are in an environment where the long-term gain is rare, it makes sense for them to maximize their reward now. Children figure that delaying gratification is not worth the emotional labor if they do not trust that gratification will ever come. It makes more sense for them to act impulsively than to self-regulate and hope to receive a payoff. Obviously, the children in the reliable group had a different experience—and a different interpretation of their options. They trusted the wait was worth it based on their life experience.

All this marshmallow eating has significant implications in the workplace. Employees are constantly appraising their workplace—evaluating if it is reliable or unreliable, safe or threatening, trustworthy or untrustworthy. An individual is much more likely to have high-quality self-regulation in a reliable, safe, and trusting work setting.

For optimal motivation, high-quality psychological needs are the endgame. High-quality self-regulation is the means.

Leaders and organizations need to be more proactive in creating a workplace where people don't have to work so hard to self-regulate.[6] Unfortunately, even the best workplaces can disappoint, engender bad feelings, promote vulnerabilities, and provoke emotions that feed people's impulse to gobble junk food—whether marshmallows, pellets, or french fries—as fast as they can.

> **For optimal motivation, high-quality psychological needs are the endgame. High-quality self-regulation is the means.**

People cannot count on the perfect workplace—but your leadership can help reduce their challenges to effectively self-regulate. By shifting out of overdrive and focusing on the MVPs of self-regulation, you can help people into the driver's seat for themselves.

The MVPs of Self-Regulation

Self-regulation is the mechanism for countering the emotional triggers and distractions that tend to undermine people's psychological needs and their optimal motivation at work. The MVPs of high-quality self-regulation are mindfulness, values, and purpose. Consider how your leadership can help your team members experience the MVPs to experience optimal motivation.

Mindfulness: The *M* of Self-Regulation's MVPs

Mindfulness is noticing—being aware and attuned to what is happening in the present moment without judgment or an automatic reaction. It is a state of being but is also a skill that requires development through practice and patience.

Every human being has the capacity for mindfulness—some more than others. I don't have what's called *dispositional mindfulness*. My personality type is quick to judge and react. My natural response to the world around me is an extroverted, direct, and fight reaction. For me, being mindful requires calming the surge of energy generated when I think my anger is justified by unfair, unjust, or what I consider stupid people, organizations, or systems. As I'm flooded with "fight" energy, I might find myself lashing out by putting others down or attacking their character. I've worked on mindfulness and realized I need daily practice to overcome the reflexive rush from self-righteous indignation of believing I am right and someone else is wrong.

People express mindless reactions differently. Some yell, rant, and bully. Others become passive-aggressive or go silent, avoiding the person or situation most responsible for thwarting their psychological needs. When we are not mindful, we tend to react with typical behavior patterns—many of which we are born with or have acquired unconsciously through life experience.

Without the skill of mindfulness, we are likely to succumb to uncontrolled emotions in the following situations:

- *An absence of choice*—We are pressured or feel a lack of control over a person or situation.
- *An absence of connection*—A person or organization has disappointed us or let us down.
- *An absence of competence*—We don't have the ability to cope effectively with the person or situation.

A lack of mindfulness leads to low-quality self-regulation and one of the three suboptimal motivational outlooks:

- *Disinterested*—Without mindfulness, people disengage because they are overwhelmed but not thoughtfully or consciously; they are unable to align the situation or what they've been asked to do with their values, purpose, or anything meaningful.
- *External*—Without mindfulness, people revel in the power they exert without awareness of better alternatives; are stimulated by their status without appreciating how they affect the inner peace of others; or are controlled by an external reward or incentive that deprives them of the positive energy, vitality, and well-being of optimal motivation.
- *Imposed*—Without mindfulness, people feel victimized and cornered without choices; they succumb to fear or pressure.

Ironically, the low-quality energy generated by suboptimal motivation can be addictive. The rush of adrenaline generated through self-righteous indignation, the heat of anger, or the thrill of the kill in intense competition can fuel a person the same way junk food does. Whether the energy is directed inwardly through passive aggression and silent disengagement or outwardly through a lack of action, frustration, or impatience, consider this: the only way to sustain negative energy is to continue fueling whatever sparked the negativity in the first place. Sustaining negative energy requires feeding negative energy. It is exhausting. And it is no way to live.

Mindfulness is highly relevant to a person's motivational outlook. Kirk Warren Brown, a leading mindfulness researcher, has proven that mindfulness and choice, connection, and competence are directly linked. In other words, when people are mindful, it is almost impossible for them *not* to experience the three psychological needs. The neuroscience of mindfulness is fascinating. Brain scans show that being mindful and experiencing choice, connection, and competence activate the same part of your brain. The more mindful you are, the more likely you are to satisfy your psychological needs.[7]

I have witnessed this outcome firsthand in motivation training sessions. Participants identify a goal where their motivational outlook is suboptimal. A learning partner poses questions to determine how choice, connection, and competence are being experienced. Almost all participants report the same phenomenon: halfway through the list of questions, they feel their motivational outlook shifting. It is remarkable to watch. The questions, posed in a nonthreatening way, enable participants to be mindfully aware. Suddenly they realize, "I do have choices; this goal is aligned to meaningful values and a sense of purpose that deepens my experience of connection; I can learn and build competence by pursuing this goal." Through mindfulness, they can experience their greatest opportunities for growth and freedom.

When people are mired in their prejudiced version of reality, they have fewer options for coping with that reality. Mindfulness provides a view of reality without the filters, self-centered thoughts, and historical conditioning that obscure options for reacting differently. A space exists between what is happening to you and the way you react to it. Mindfulness is that space, one where you can choose how to respond.

When we teach individuals the skill of motivation, they learn how to use mindfulness as a tool for shifting their motivational outlook. They come to appreciate how the energy they generate from a suboptimal motivational outlook pales in comparison to the vitality they generate through an optimal motivational outlook.

When a person is mindful, she experiences a heightened sense of choice because she is not controlled by her own potentially misconstrued and misaligned self-concept based on irrelevant past experiences. In this mindful state, a person is better able to experience connection because she is genuinely concerned about another person without self-serving interpretations or prejudice. Mindfulness also enhances her competence because, free from a knee-jerk reaction, she's aware of options to make more appropriate choices—she is more resilient and capable of navigating the challenges she faces.

Your leadership responsibility is to create mindful moments for those you lead. I hope you'll find chapters 4 and 5 relevant and practical—they recommend specific leadership skills to promote mindfulness and people's experience of choice, connection, and competence. But chapter 6 addresses what may be your greatest challenge—it reminds you that before you can promote mindfulness in others, you first need to experience optimal motivation yourself.

Values: The *V* of Self-Regulation's MVPs

Values are premeditated, cognitive standards of what a person considers good, bad, worse, better, or best. Values are enduring beliefs people have chosen to accept as guidelines for how they work—and live their lives.

Values are at the heart of high-quality self-regulation, yet most individuals have not explored their own work-related values. I find this ironic. If you stop people in the hallway at work and ask them to list their organization's values, purpose, or mission statement, chances are they will come close. Today, promoting organizational values and purpose is an accepted business practice. This is a good thing. However, we cannot stop there. Individuals need to identify, develop, clarify, declare, and operationalize their own work-related values and purpose—and then determine how they align with the organization's values.[8]

Employees with clarified values are more likely to experience high-quality self-regulation despite inevitable workplace demands and challenges. But therein lies the problem. First, people need to have developed values! If values are mechanisms for change and good decision-making, shouldn't all individuals in the organization have clarity about their own values—and how they align, or not, with the organization's values?

A theme of this book is that motivating people doesn't work because they are already motivated; they are always motivated. What matters is the quality of their motivation. The same is true of values. People are always acting from their values; what matters is the quality of their values.

Developing workplace values for yourself and with your people is worth the investment of time. Linking developed values to a challenging task, goal, or situation activates a shift between a suboptimal motivational outlook and optimal motivational outlook. A developed value is freely chosen from alternatives, with an understanding of the consequences of the alternatives. It is prized and cherished and acted upon over time.

An intriguing aspect of values is that developing them tends to be a mindful process that reflects not only what we need to flourish but what others need as well. Acting upon developed values helps us satisfy our psychological needs.

To guide your people's shift to an optimal motivational outlook, help them self-regulate by linking assigned tasks, goals, or projects to their own developed values. For you to do that, your people need to have developed values—and to have you as a good role model.

Purpose: The *P* of Self-Regulation's MVPs

Purpose is a deep and meaningful reason for doing something. Living your purpose is acting with a noble intention—when your actions are infused with social significance.

As consultant and author Dr. Charles Garfield drove over the San Francisco–Oakland Bay Bridge on his way to work, he heard loud music coming from the tollbooth he was about to enter. He rolled down his window to pay his toll and found a dancing tollbooth operator. "I'm having a party," the operator declared. Garfield drove away more joyful than he did most mornings and realized he had just experienced a peak-performing tollbooth operator.

Intrigued, Garfield followed up and discovered that the young man's purpose was to be a dancer. His coworkers described their booths as "vertical coffins," but this young man saw his booth as a stage for performing and his job as an opportunity to dance. He developed a philosophy about his job, created an environment to support his vision, and happened to entertain those he served.[9] Research on peak performers confirms what you might suspect about people who attain high levels of success and sustain it over time. Peak performers are not goal-driven. They are values-based and inspired by a noble purpose.

> Peak performers are not goal-driven.
> They are values-based and inspired
> by a noble purpose.

The danger of drive is that it distracts people from what truly makes them dance. People are more likely to meet or exceed expectations when they pursue goals within a context of a meaningful purpose. If, for some reason, the dancing toll-booth operator were failing to achieve his goals of collecting correct fees and preventing backups on the bridge, as his manager, you would know the root of the problem: his work-related role, values, and purpose are not synched. However, odds are that this peak performer is achieving both your goals and his personal, purpose-based goals.

Employees who have clarified their personal values and vision and integrated them with their organization's stated values and vision are likely to be living, working, and even dancing purposefully. They are less likely to look to you or others to drive their behavior.

Most organizations have a vision, mission, or purpose statement, but few employees have one for their work-related role. This is a lost opportunity and a shame. Without a noble purpose, what is enticing employees away from the daily bombardment of junk foods? Without a higher cause or sense of meaning, why give up those french fries or wait for the promised marshmallow?

Collaborate with your employees to align their perception of their role-related values and purpose and your perception. Come to conclusions together that meet both their needs and those of the organization. Acting with a noble purpose is a sure path to high-quality self-regulation.

Case in Point: Mohammedan and the iPad Mini

Imagine three hundred pharmaceutical reps from the Middle East and Africa vying to win an iPad Mini. The instructions were easy: Everyone stands up. I flip a coin. While the coin is in the air, everyone shouts out either heads or tails. If you guess wrong, you sit down. If you guess correctly, you stay standing for the next round. The rounds continue until only one person is left standing. That person wins the iPad Mini.

The winner was Mohammedan from Egypt, who was so excited about winning the iPad Mini that he bounded on stage to grab it, along with my microphone. It turns out Mohammedan was a pharmaceutical rep by day and a singer by night. He started singing in Arabic. All of a sudden, three hundred people were standing and singing with him—he sang a line; they responded with the same line. It was electric!

After the frivolity died down, I explained the Spectrum of Motivation model, relating it to how they experienced the heads-or-tails activity. We explored the horizontal axis of psychological needs and how all humans, regardless of culture, creed, race, gender, or generation, experience positive and sustainable energy, vitality, and a sense of well-being when their needs for choice, connection, and competence are satisfied. We explored the vertical axis of self-regulation. We did activities practicing how they could use the MVPs of mindfulness, values, and purpose to shift from a suboptimal motivational outlook to an optimal motivational outlook.

Things were going well until, during the lunch break, the general manager of the region approached me: "Susan, we have a problem. Mohammedan cheated." "What do you mean, he cheated?" "He stayed standing even when he called out the wrong answer. He wants to return the iPad. What are we going to do?" The GM was distraught, and I felt a sinking sensation. But then, I realized we had a wonderful opportunity.

I approached Mohammedan with an idea that he nervously agreed to: tell the group how he was feeling and what he had learned. He returned to the stage. He had written out his confession on paper. His hands were shaking as he read it aloud. He was full of emotion as he explained his external motivational outlook during the heads-or-tails activity. He admitted wanting to win the iPad Mini but also being driven to impress his colleagues and be the star of the moment.

Mohammedan related his surprise at how miserable he felt despite winning the iPad Mini. He described how, in a mindful moment, he became aware of his low-quality self-regulation and that he had failed to live up to the organization's values, or his own, for honesty and integrity. He realized that winning through cheating had not satisfied his psychological needs for choice, connection, and competence. He wanted to return the iPad Mini so someone more deserving would have it.

Then something amazing happened. Mohammedan again had three hundred people standing and cheering—but this time for a very different reason. People were moved to tears. I was one of them. Mohammedan was experiencing high-quality energy, vitality, and well-being that generated a positive ripple effect among hundreds in that room. That moment was a glorious demonstration of shifting out of overdrive through high-quality self-regulation. The result was optimal motivation—for the entire group, not just Mohammedan.

Recapping "Shifting Out of Overdrive"

The danger of drive is that it promotes suboptimal motivation that diminishes people's psychological need for choice, connection, and competence. Drivers come in tangible forms, such as money, incentives, and a big office or title, and intangible forms, such as approval, status, shame, and fear.

When employees focus on an external driver, they are controlled by it or whoever is doing the driving. People ultimately resent leaders who create a pressurized workplace that erodes their sense of choice.

Research indicates that people regard managers who drive for results as self-serving. They consider support by these managers as conditional: "If you do as I say, then I will reward you in some way." Conditional support thwarts people's sense of connection.

Driving for results by adding pressure and tension blocks people's creativity and ability to focus, leaving them feeling inadequate or ineffective at coping with the circumstances—which undermines people's sense of competence.

Leaders can shift out of overdrive by promoting the MVPs of high-quality self-regulation: mindfulness, values, and purpose.

4

If Motivating People Doesn't Work ... What Does?

Motivating people doesn't work. But that doesn't stop many well-meaning, beleaguered, and desperate managers from influencing (bribing? manipulating?) people with rewards, pressure, tension, fear, threats, or guilt. Still, some leaders understand the limitations of external and imposed motivation—they recognize that motivation is an inside-out phenomenon. Then they take a giant leap in the wrong direction. They assume they can tap into people's intrinsic motivation by asking, "What motivates you?" Big mistake. I urge you to refrain from asking people to identify a source of a longing they probably don't understand.

People usually don't realize that the "something" at the core of their dissatisfaction is their unmet psychological need for choice (autonomy), connection (meaningful relationships and work), and competence (growth, learning, opportunities, and resources).

Without insight into the true nature of motivation, people tend to naively answer the question "What motivates you?" in suboptimal ways. Based on cultural or societal norms, they cite the usual suspects: more money, power, status, acquisitions, popularity, perks, and benefits.

It should be noted that some desires, such as money or leisure time, might reflect optimal motivation if aligned with meaningful values such as family and health. Evidence from current research suggests that Gen Z employees cite leaving jobs because they don't offer flexibility, meaningful work, or opportunities for growth.[1] But leaving their need-thwarting jobs doesn't mean they understand how to seek need-fulfilling jobs. The following chapter explores this phenomenon in more depth.

The truth is that no matter your generation, most people still depend on external motivation to compensate for their missing psychological needs. As you might recall from chapter 2, the scientific term for this phenomenon is *compensatory need satisfaction*. And it doesn't work.

You're probably thinking, "If motivating people doesn't work, and people don't understand what motivates them, what can I do?" You can't motivate anyone, but as a leader, you can create an environment where people are more likely to experience optimal motivation. That means facilitating their need for choice, connection, and competence through three leadership capacities.

Compare traditional leadership competencies and behaviors with leadership capacities that promote optimal motivation in table 4.1.

TABLE 4.1 Traditional competencies compared to foundational leadership capacities

Traditional competencies and behaviors that undermine people's optimal motivation	Foundational leadership capacities that facilitate people's optimal motivation
• Drive results • Apply pressure to win • Hold people accountable (rather than encouraging personal accountability) • Rely on incentives	• Encourage choice (autonomy) by helping people realize that they always have choices, have options within boundaries, and are the source of their actions
• Avoid emotion • Focus on metrics without aligning to values • Discount interpersonal relationships • Push hot buttons • Reward results over effort • Praise	• Deepen connection (relatedness) by helping people feel a sense of belonging and genuine connection to others without concerns about ulterior motives, aligning goals and actions to meaningful values and a sense of purpose and contributing to something greater than themselves
• Focus on outcome goals while discounting learning goals • Punish mistakes • Wield knowledge and expertise power	• Build competence by helping people feel effective at managing everyday situations, demonstrating skill over time, and experiencing growth and learning

Your Leadership Capacity Is Essential to People's Optimal Motivation

In his groundbreaking book *Why We Do What We Do*, Dr. Edward Deci shares a compelling example of a medical doctor who applied his leadership capacity to encourage choice, deepen connection, and build competence.[2]

A doctor instructed an elderly woman to take two pills every morning, warning her of dire consequences if she didn't. She would comply for a couple of months, then stop and end up in the emergency room. Doctors and nurses reminded her to take her medication, often reprimanding her for taking resources away from others who needed emergency care. Her family admonished her for scaring them each time they discovered she was at the hospital again.

After years of suffering the repetitive behavior, the woman's nephew noted that recently his aunt seemed to have mastered her medicine-taking issue. When he asked her what had changed, she reported finding a new doctor she liked. She said the doctor took time to talk to her about her medications and trips to the emergency ward on her first visit. She confessed to him that she simply forgot to take the pills each morning. When the doctor asked her if there was a better time to take her medications, she told him about her lifetime routine of drinking warm milk before bed. The doctor explained that it didn't matter when she took the pills and that dairy wouldn't interfere with the medication, so if she preferred to take the pills before bed with her warm milk, that was fine. She hadn't been to the emergency room since.

Think about what the new doctor did. He guided his patient's realization that she had options and encouraged her to make a choice. He deepened connection by taking the time to talk with her and demonstrated he cared about her trips to the emergency room for her own well-being and the benefit of others, including her family, who worried about her. And he built her competence by providing the information she needed to make the right choice. His leadership made it more likely for the elderly woman to experience choice, connection, and competence; change her behavior; and form a positive habit that literally saved her life.

What does it mean to be a leader if not to help people flourish and excel—so they thrive, not merely survive? A sad reality is that most organizations hold leaders accountable for competencies defined by six top-down management theories published between 1841 and 1972.[3] Instead of embracing contemporary motivation science, leaders are still trying to motivate people using tactics based on B. F. Skinner's animal studies, Abraham Maslow's outdated hierarchy, and David McClelland's power-centric principles.[4] Never has there been a better time to upskill leaders on the foundational leadership capacities that simultaneously promote people's well-being and their workplace performance.

That's why I'm intrigued with this operational definition of leadership (meaning that each part of the definition is substantiated empirically) by Dr. Drea Zigarmi: leadership is the act of arousing, engaging, and satisfying the motives of the followers—in an environment of conflict, competition, or change—that results in the followers taking a course of action toward a mutually shared vision.[5]

People's most fundamental motives are the three basic psychological needs required for optimal motivation. Your leadership either promotes or thwarts people's experience of those needs.[6] You have choices about how you lead. You can keep doing what you've always done—and get the results you've always gotten. You can mimic what you see other leaders doing, good and bad, and hope for better instead of worse. Or you can elevate your leadership by taking advantage of groundbreaking motivation science so people are more likely to experience optimal motivation, achieve their goals, and thrive at work.

Three Foundational Leadership Capacities

Everyone relishes experiencing optimal motivation. Yet, as I've written throughout this book, this state is fragile. External pressures are constantly enticing people into suboptimal motivation. I'm reminded of the movie *The Godfather Part III*. The story's protagonist, Michael Corleone, has endeavored for years to legitimize the family business. In his frustration at the people and circumstances thwarting his efforts, Michael, played by Al Pacino, utters the dramatic line that resonated with so many: "Just when I thought I was out, they pull me back in."

Your leadership may be the most potent force preventing people from getting sucked into the vortex of suboptimal motivation. You can't compel people to thrive, but you can pave the way for them to experience—and sustain—optimal motivation. That means embracing the foundational leadership capacities to encourage choice, deepen connection, and build competence.

Embrace a philosophy instead of a to-do list. Imagine if you mastered the three leadership capacities. That would be grand! But let me suggest a potentially grander plan. Instead of committing to a to-do list for mastering motivation with others, I urge you to embrace a philosophy. Commit to reflective awareness. Notice how your leadership affects people's experience of choice, connection, and competence. Ask yourself these questions during or after an interaction with someone you lead: Am I encouraging choice, or did I just erode it? Am I deepening connection, or did I just thwart it? Am I building competence, or did I just undermine it?

The skills you're about to learn can lessen the eroding, thwarting, and undermining of people's psychological needs.[7] But none of us are perfect all the time. I know this from personal experience. Yesterday, I blocked out time to write. The day was unusually hot, but rather than turn on the air conditioner, I flung the doors open and turned on the house fan. My younger brother dropped by to help fix a landscaping problem and shut the doors, thinking he was doing me a favor. The problem is that the house fan requires airflow. When I heard a strange roar coming from the fan, instead of alleviating the issue by reopening the doors, I found my brother and asked in an accusatory tone if he'd closed the doors. Irritated by being distracted from my work, I informed him: "I had the doors open on purpose for the fan—it needs air for circulating!"

My brother explained that he was making a lot of noise outside and closed the doors, thinking he was doing me a favor. I could have left it there. But in a moment of reflection, I realized something my brother didn't consciously perceive: by accusing him of making a bad decision, I threatened his sense of choice. Would he be inhibited from taking the initiative to do what he thinks is helpful in the future? By pouncing on him without seeking out his side of the story, I threatened his sense of connection. Would he be more inclined to tiptoe around me in the future? By questioning his judgment, I had threatened his sense of competence. Would he be less trusting of his own judgment in the future?

Even though we have a long history together, I regretted treating a family member with less respect than I'd treat a team member I manage in the workplace. I hadn't applied the three leadership capacities with my brother, but recognizing the lost opportunity for encouraging choice, deepening connection, and building competence, I decided to do it retroactively.

I grabbed a fresh peach, a fruit I know he loves, and delivered it to him with a message: "I wish I hadn't snapped at you about the doors. You couldn't have known the situation and only did what you thought was best—as you typically do. I want you to know how much I appreciate your help around the house, and at the end of the day, I trust your judgment."

At first, he looked at me quizzically. Then he nodded and replied, "You know how grateful I am for your support." When he left for the day, he shouted, "I love you, sis." You may think this vignette is silly or insignificant, especially since it came from an everyday interaction that lasted only minutes. But I beg to differ. The quality of our life depends on the quality of our relationships. That truth is as relevant in the workplace as it is in our personal life.

My imperfections give me plenty of opportunities to practice reflective awareness. I've become more sensitive about how my leadership affects the quality of other people's motivation. As you practice the three leadership capacities, appreciate that you may not always get it right, but with mindful leadership, you can make it right.

Mastering the First Leadership Capacity: Encourage Choice

To encourage choice, help people realize that they always have choices, have options within boundaries, and are the source of their actions.

To encourage choice, help people realize that they always have choices, have options within boundaries, and are the source of their actions.

Do you question the practicality of offering people choices? What about job requirements, legalities, and nonnegotiables? What if people have to follow safety protocols, federal regulations, and compliance standards?

Take heart. When you encourage choice, you aren't just allowing people to do what they want. Encouraging choice promotes a person's *perception* of autonomy, control, and volition.

One of the most potent examples of experiencing choice despite a lack of freedom is Dr. Viktor Frankl's account of how he and others managed to survive unimaginable horrors in a World War II concentration camp. As a prisoner of war, Frankl had no freedoms accorded to him. His book *Man's Search for Meaning* profoundly describes how he fulfilled his basic need for choice by choosing to appreciate a beautiful sunrise, help others suffering more than he, and accept responsibility for his frame of mind. Of that experience, he wrote, "Everything can be taken from a man but one thing: the last of the human freedoms—to choose one's attitude in any given set of circumstances, to choose one's own way."[8]

Encouraging choice doesn't mean giving people freedom—that implies you control them and their actions. Instead, you offer people an opportunity to escape being prisoners of their own thoughts. You help them fulfill their essential need for autonomy.

Could You Be Eroding People's Need for Choice?

When you drive for results, you may think that applying pressure or micromanaging seems like a commonsense solution. But unless the situation is dire, avoid choice-eroding leadership behaviors, including any of the following:

- Relying on incentives and rewards to motivate
- Applying pressure to drive results or win
- Not allowing another person to speak by doing most of the talking yourself
- Not offering options because you're in a hurry
- Micromanaging
- Wielding your position or expertise power to punish people or coerce decisions
- Failing to ask for input on decisions when the person has the competence to provide worthwhile insight and ideas
- Promoting your personal values without consideration that other people's values might be different than yours

- Stifling mindfulness through closed-ended questions and controlling language

The final item on the list can provoke a bit of controversy. I urge leaders to mind their language, for words can generate negative energy that contributes to people feeling unsafe, defensive, guarded, inferior, incompetent, or fearful. Then, I provide an example using two statements communicating a deadline. The first version uses controlling language that tends to erode the person's perception of choice:

"Your deadline is next week. You must do whatever it takes and push harder to finish this on time."

The second version uses noncontrolling language that encourages the individual to come to his or her own conclusions about how to achieve this goal:

"Your deadline is next week. If you're feeling pressure or concerned that you might not make it, let's explore solutions to help you meet expectations and relieve the source of your tension."

Often, managers reject my recommendation: "Why should I have to guard every word I utter to protect someone's perception of choice?" They complain about a workforce of "snowflakes"—a derogatory slang term implying a generation of employees with an inflated sense of uniqueness and an unwarranted sense of entitlement. They have little respect for a workforce they consider overly emotional, easily offended, and unable to deal with opposing opinions.

But, if I may say a few words about words, language defines a culture. The Japanese language includes at least six ways to represent rice, and just one of the Inuit dialects has fifty words for snow.[9] Language is a living thing, constantly evolving and reflecting societal changes. For example, in the 1960s, when you thought a person did something stupid, it was common to call them "retarded." I was offended by the term because my sister, Terri, was born with water on the brain from spina bifida. My heart broke when she was old enough to understand the word and regretfully claimed, "I'm retarded." She *was* physically and mentally disabled. But a massive distinction exists between the terms used in a medical diagnosis and the judgment that accompanied society's careless use of the word. Today, thanks to greater awareness and empathy, most people refrain from thoughtlessly calling someone retarded.

I know the current antiwoke movement paints such evolutions in our language with a broad stroke—claiming newer generations of too-sensitive people are acting as the "language police." Of course, in any societal change, overzealous advocates can push too far in their righteousness. But the diversity, equity, and inclusion movement reflects a growing awareness of the minorities and subcultures who have borne the brunt of our ignorance for too long.

How does all this play into the words you use as a leader when promoting people's autonomy? The language of business harbors vestiges of traditional command-and-control leadership and a leader-centric perspective proven inadequate for promoting well-being and workplace effectiveness.

The following chapter delves deeper into other cultural and societal changes affecting how leaders lead. If you don't want to erode people's psychological need for choice, it's time to avoid language and practices reflecting top-down power and control—and an outdated cultural model.

How to Encourage Choice

Let go of your fear that people can't handle choices. Ensure your language reflects an openness to diverse thoughts and approaches and embrace the significance of autonomy as central to people's well-being. Consider practicing these two leadership skills proven to encourage choice:

- Explore options within boundaries.
- Present goals and timelines as valuable information.

Explore Options within Boundaries

I was asked to deal with the fallout from a situation that rocked the sales department of a prominent pharmaceutical company. All the sales representatives had been warned not to cut and paste drug studies to impress doctors with their drug's efficacy. The reps knew that noncompliance with the law would endanger the company and get them fired. But the pressure to sell was so fierce that three highly regarded sales representatives breached the federal protocols by improperly presenting clinical studies to doctors. They were fired straightaway.

I asked a manager to demonstrate a typical conversation with a sales rep to reinforce federal guidelines. As might be expected, the conversation was one-way and direct:

> When selling our drug, you must adhere to the strict federal protocol described in this memo. For example, you cannot pull out quotes and present them out of context.

You have to present the entire study. If you go beyond these guidelines, you face immediate termination.

The "conversation" didn't take long.

Then the managers and I collaboratively prepared a conversation starter using a different approach to encourage choice and avoid eroding the sales representative's sense of autonomy:

> I know you are eager to increase your sales. We can discuss strategies for doing that while also adhering to the strict federal protocols for selling our drugs. You need to stay within these boundaries to protect your client, yourself, our company—and, most importantly, the patient receiving the drug. Within these limits, however, you still have options. You can make choices and decisions that will affect your relationship with the doctor, the quality of your proposals, and the effectiveness of your sales efforts. Let's explore your options for selling this product within the stated boundaries.

Spelling out the rules of engagement is a common management practice. But managers rarely discuss the options people have within boundaries that promote (legal) creativity and innovative thinking. This type of conversation requires a leader to be more thoughtful and it takes more time. But more importantly, when you invite choice within boundaries, you promote your team member's optimal motivation. The payoff is immediate and sustainable when you are not around to dangle a carrot or wield a stick.

Present Goals and Timelines as Valuable Information

When I was nine years old, I began writing a book. I knew from the first sentence that it was lousy, so I abandoned it. But I never stopped dreaming of being an author. I finally realized the dream thirty-seven years later. Today I've authored or coauthored nine books, if you count the one you're reading now, with six different publishers. Despite my love of writing, not all my experiences lived up to the dream. Working with publishers has ranged from painful to exhilarating.

The painful publishers dictated hard deadlines for submitting the manuscript. I had no choice in the book's final title or cover design. Editors demanded changes I disagreed with. As deadlines loomed, the pressure affected the quality of my work and life. I felt guilty watching a movie or going out with friends. My day job began to suffer because of the stress I felt when not working on the book.

Enter Berrett-Koehler (BK), the publisher of this and two of my previous books. BK needs to establish hard deadlines for manuscripts too. But it takes a radically different approach to working with its authors. The publisher invited me to an Author's Day to meet the people responsible for getting my book into the hands of readers. I was inspired by a catered lunch where employees and guests came to hear my intentions and an overview of the book. I attended scheduled meetings with every team that shared responsibility for getting the book out of my head and to readers. The groups described and explained their timelines for production and clarified their expectations—along with my role in making it all happen. Rather than feeling pressured, I was optimally motivated to play my part in a collaborative effort. I have been living my nine-year-old self's dream ever since.

BK is a master at communicating deadlines, schedules, requirements, and expectations as data or information necessary for achieving agreed-upon outcomes. You can communicate expectations directly, like this:

> You need to submit your final report no later than July 20.

Or, instead, communicate a deadline as a piece of valuable information that encourages choice, like this:

> This project needs to be completed by July 20 so the CFO has time to review it before the board meeting on August 15. I created a spreadsheet to propose a timeline so that all team members understand their role and can schedule their time appropriately. After you've had a chance to review the timeline, let me know if you foresee steps I haven't included. Alert me to challenges I haven't considered that might influence your ability to complete the report by July 20.

People are less likely to feel controlled by external or imposed motivation when you frame your message as valuable information or knowledge that will help them succeed.

Mastering the Second Leadership Capacity: Deepen Connection

To deepen connection, help people feel a sense of belonging and genuine connection to others without concerns about ulterior motives, align goals and actions to meaningful values and a sense of purpose, and contribute to something greater than themselves.

If you join me at the front of the room during a presentation to executives, you will witness a fascinating phenomenon when I reveal a slide of a baby named Braelyn. The leaders have no idea who Braelyn is or why her photo is on the screen. But you feel their energy shift.

I describe what I see to the audience: their expressions are softened, and some smile. "What's happening right now?" I ask them. They speculate: "She's cute." "She's reaching out, and it makes me want to respond." "She reminds me of my daughter." I urge them to examine what they are feeling. Finally, someone dares to admit what it is: unconditional love. They realize how drawn they are to the purity of Braelyn's intention—she's reaching out for no other reason than to connect. That is what they are responding to. It feels good when someone wants to connect without an ulterior motive.

Braelyn's photo represents a basic psychological need that every human being has for connection—the need to care about and be cared about by others without ulterior motives.

We know humans thrive when all three psychological needs for choice, connection, and competence are satisfied. However, the need for connection is often discounted or nonexistent in workplaces. This absence is a considerable risk because if people aren't getting their need for connection met at work, there's a chance they are not getting it met at all, given the amount of time people spend at work compared to other areas of their life. Without connection at work, people will not thrive or have the energy, vitality, and well-being required for pursuing and achieving their goals.

Could You Be Eroding People's Need for Connection?

Do you avoid the dreaded *F* word—*feelings*—at work? It's common practice to diminish their importance in the workplace. I explore this misguided notion in later chapters. Still, I want to provide a research-based argument for why you need to pay attention to people's feelings—especially if you're going to help fulfill their need for connection.

We know that people appraise the world around them cognitively (through their thinking) and affectively (through their emotions).[10] For example, we constantly appraise our environment to determine whether we are under threat or safe, excited or bored, or positive or negative. We conclude that we're experiencing either well-being or ill-being through our thoughts and feelings. But, in the end, our emotions have the most influence on the outcome of our appraisal.

When people's appraisal leads to a sense of well-being, they exhibit five intentions representing work passion, the upper end of employee engagement. According to cutting-edge research by the Employee Work Passion Company, people intend to do the following:

- Stay in the organization.
- Perform at above-standard expectations.
- Endorse the organization to others.
- Use discretionary time on behalf of the organization.
- Demonstrate organizational citizenship behaviors.[11]

These intentions are the most significant predictors of the behavior that distinguishes employee work passion from employee disengagement.

My question to you is: Why discount or avoid people's feelings when their emotions are core to the appraisal process that determines whether they experience well-being or ill-being and employee work passion or disengagement?

Even if you appreciate the significance of emotions at work, you could unwittingly be thwarting people's psychological need for connection by

- Avoiding emotions and feelings
- Not being transparent
- Believing that vulnerability is a weakness
- Not listening
- Focusing on metrics without providing a rationale
- Promoting results and rewards over values
- Failing to align goals to a higher purpose
- Judging rather than empathizing
- Praising rather than expressing gratitude

How to Deepen Connection

You might notice a theme in this list of leader behaviors that undermine connection between you and the people you lead:

a lack of compassion. Compassion is the demonstration of empathetically caring about someone beyond your own self-interest. Studies on compassion include factors such as kindness versus indifference, common humanity versus separation, and mindfulness versus disengagement. (For more information on compassionate leadership, visit centerforcompassionate leadersip.org/research-papers.)

To demonstrate connection when a crisis arises at work, notice the nature of people's complaints and demands. Do they begin asking for money to implement your initiatives? If so, it could be a sign they are suboptimally motivated and reverting to external rewards for the sugar high that comes with junk-food motivation. But also notice your reaction. When people respond negatively to your demands, do you react with kindness, acknowledge the common humanity of the situation, and mindfully explore options? Or do you drive forward with indifference, separate your emotions from your actions, and disengage in the name of progress?

As I write this book, Elon Musk's Twitter takeover dominates the news. I have no idea how the situation will play out, but Musk's leadership appears ineffective and destructive. He gave his employees an ultimatum: stay at Twitter only if you're willing to commit to "long hours" at a "high intensity" and be "extremely hardcore," which resulted in hundreds of people leaving. Desperate business realities may be driving Musk's tactics. But it's not just what you do as a leader that matters; it's also how you do it.

With over 50 percent of the Twitter workforce gone over the course of two weeks through insensitively communicated layoffs and employees choosing to escape the chaos (and hundreds more who would leave if they could afford to, Musk seems to be cutting his nose to spite his face.

One of his tweets may reveal part of Musk's motivation. He posted, "How do you make a small fortune in social media? Start out with a large one." Is Musk beating himself up over a wrongheaded (suboptimally motivated) business deal? His feelings about himself may guide how he treats others.

Research highlights how a lack of self-compassion can lead to a lack of compassion for others. Self-compassion is being open to one's own suffering—not avoiding and disconnecting from it. If you are suffering, self-compassion is the ability to heal yourself with kindness.

Unfortunately, many top executives suffer from alexithymia—the inability to identify and describe the emotions they are experiencing. Too many executives have risen to positions of power marked by dysfunction in emotional awareness, social attachment, and interpersonal relating. Without the ability to recognize and cope with their emotions, executives fall prey to fatal distractions, such as money, power, and status, that lead to a lack of well-being. If leaders aren't flourishing, there's a good chance the people they lead are languishing.

When you consider the leadership capacity to deepen connection, keep in mind that the person most in need of that connection may be you.

You have so many opportunities to deepen connection each day. You can demonstrate empathy by listening intentionally, be more transparent, share the rationale for goals, reveal information about yourself and the organization relevant to the situation, and openly discuss your intentions. You can also experiment with two leadership skills proven to increase connection dramatically:

- Align work with values and purpose.
- Replace external motivation with meaning.

Align Work with Values and Purpose

Have you had a values conversation with the people you lead? Do you know what they find meaningful? Have you helped them make the connection between their daily efforts, values they personally hold dear, and a noble purpose?

You have the opportunity to deepen connection by aligning people's work with values and purpose every day. When you share departmental goals, explain how they link to the organization's purpose. In one-on-one conversations, help individuals align their goals to their personal values and purpose. Facilitate a discussion with your team on how their work contributes to the company's stakeholders. Talk to people about their personal concerns during a change initiative before trying to sell them on why the change is a good idea for the company. And always advocate for justice and transparency—especially concerning access to resources and opportunities.

> **You have the opportunity to deepen connection by aligning people's work with values and purpose every day.**

Replace External Motivation with Meaning

Depending on external rewards to motivate (or manipulate) people's behavior is a twofold tragedy.

The first tragedy is that dangling rewards to get people to do your bidding relegates people to the status of a show animal—like a monkey forced to do tricks for treats.

In 2016, we finally realized the inhumane treatment of circus elephants and banned them from circuses in the United States.[12] We know how paying for performance works out for animals. Why do we think this practice is appropriate for humans? Even this seemingly innocuous suggestion can erode people's connection to a more meaningful reason for achieving their goal: "If you really focus on closing business over the next couple of weeks, you can still make your bonus and qualify for the sales trip."

Pushing external rewards as the reason to take action almost always results in people experiencing suboptimal motivation.

The second tragedy is that you distract people from more profound and meaningful reasons for pursuing their goals.

I had assigned participants attending a self leadership workshop to rank a list of workplace motivators. Each group was challenged to come to a consensus on their list, then compare their group's answers with research findings. One group couldn't come to an agreement because Sonny refused to agree that "interesting work" should be the top motivator. He was convinced that people's number one workplace motivator was "money."

Sonny explained, "I know you said that research shows that money is not the best reason to be motivated, but to be honest, it's my reason, and I'm not going to apologize for it. I think most people would agree with me."

Sonny became the first person I attempted to publicly guide through the process of understanding the true nature of motivation. He didn't know the Spectrum of Motivation, the six motivational outlooks, or the three psychological needs. But based on his reaction to the activity and his comment, it seemed an opportune moment to experiment with techniques I was developing to help people better understand their motivation. I explained the situation to Sonny, and he graciously agreed to go along with my questions. The conversation went something like this:

Susan: Sonny, there are no right or wrong answers. I hope you feel curious about the difference in your rankings rather than judged. You claim that money is what gets you up to go to work every day. You were the only group member who listed money as the top motivator. Would you be open to investigating that?

Sonny: Sure.

Susan: Okay, I will ask you questions to explore your motivation. If it gets to be too much, just let me know. Why is money what gets you going each day?

Sonny: I just graduated from college, and I'm broke. I need money! That's why I went into sales—to make money.

Susan: That's understandable. Why is money so important to you?

Sonny: Because I need to buy things!

Susan: Why is buying things so important to you?

Sonny: Because I need things, like a new car.

Susan: Why is the new car so important?

Sonny: Because the one I have now is old and run-down. It doesn't scream *success*. I need a new car to impress people.

Susan: Why is it so crucial for you to impress people?

Sonny: Because I want them to see me as successful.

Susan: Why is it so important for people to see you as successful?

Sonny paused and, full of emotion, shared that he was the first and only person from his family to ever attend and graduate from college. His parents had sacrificed and worked multiple jobs to support him through those four years. He wanted to be successful as a testament to their sacrifice and caring. To clarify whether Sonny was feeling an imposed or aligned motivational outlook, I asked these questions:

Do you think your parents supported your college education so you could make lots of money?

Do you think your parents have expectations tied to your making a lot of money?

Do you think your parents will be disappointed if you don't make a lot of money?

Do you think your parents might love you less if you don't make lots of money?

Suddenly, Sonny got it. He realized that his interpretation of success was making lots of money. But his purpose was not about money. He worked hard every day because he was grateful for his parents, who had selflessly supported him, and he appreciated the opportunities before him. It was not about payback, obligation, or duty. It was about pure connection.

A big aha moment for Sonny was that the money and car he wanted might be by-products. He still wanted them, but he got in touch with how focusing on external rewards distracted him from values he held dear. His values and noble purpose imparted more rewarding reasons for getting out of bed each morning. Sonny wondered aloud: "What would get me out of bed after I got the car I wanted?" He concluded that love was more fulfilling and sustaining than grasping for material goods.

You can't manipulate other people's understanding of why they do what they do. But you can shift your focus from pushing incentives and rewards to facilitating a conversation about their values that enables them to connect to what's meaningful to them.

Mastering the Third Leadership Capacity: Build Competence

To build competence, help people feel effective at managing everyday situations, demonstrate skill over time, and experience growth and learning.

> To build competence, help people
> feel effective at managing everyday
> situations, demonstrate skill over time,
> and experience growth and learning.

In her book *Mindset*, Carol Dweck asserts: "People are all born with a love of learning, but a fixed mindset can undo it."[13] Dweck and her Stanford research validate our foundational need for competence. But you can also observe a toddler who tries to fulfill his insatiable curiosity and need to learn by incessantly asking you, "Why?"

A technique I encourage leaders to try is simple: in addition to asking for a progress report or a list of the week's achievements, ask your team members what they learned that would help them be more effective next week.

Elena, who attended a workshop on motivation I was teaching in Bucharest, Romania, tried the technique—although not in a way I anticipated. On the second day of the course, Elena shared her experience from the night before. She put this question to her ten-year-old son: "So what did you learn today that you thought was interesting or that you don't want to forget?"

Elena said her son rolled his eyes and retorted, "Mom, that's a stupid question. We didn't have school today, so I didn't learn anything!" Elena said she was stunned. "Here I am attending a two-day seminar that I'm paying for myself because my company doesn't cover training costs. That's how much I value learning. But when my son told me he didn't learn because there was no school that day, I realized I had failed to impart my value of learning to him."

I asked Elena how she handled the situation.

Elena said, "We sat down and talked about our values for learning! He agreed that you could learn anywhere, not just in school. If I hadn't asked him what he'd learned that day, we would never have had that conversation. I never considered having a values conversation with a ten-year-old. But it was one of the best discussions we've ever had." Elena said she and her son decided to discuss what they'd both learned at the end of each week.

Elena's conversation with her son about the value of learning broke through his potential fixed mindset, tapping into his natural proclivity for competence. I urge you to consider how your leadership interactions build or undermine people's growth mindset.

Could You Be Eroding People's Need for Competence?

You may endorse the concept of a learning organization and strive for continuous improvement. Yet you might also unintentionally undermine people's growth and learning by underestimating your role in facilitating people's psychological need for competence. Even the most well-meaning leaders erode people's competence by

- Emphasizing performance goals over learning goals
- Discounting training
- Neglecting people's development
- Assuming general competence without realizing that mastery evolves over time, especially when learning

a new skill or applying transferable skills in a new way
- Failing to acknowledge progress
- Focusing on mistakes rather than lessons learned
- Expecting perfection and not tolerating the learning curve
- Wielding knowledge and expertise power
- Failing to promote a growth mindset

Sadly, some leaders don't believe in training and development. They adhere to the throw-them-in-the-lake school of leadership. If employees sink, they aren't up to the job. If they learn to swim, then all's well. What a foolish waste of time, energy, resources, and opportunity. I don't know how you can be an effective leader without valuing growth and learning. That goes for soft skills as much as the hard skills demanded by a job. Instead, find innovative learning opportunities.

Another effective way to undermine competence is perpetuating a workplace culture where people are afraid of being judged as lazy or unproductive if caught reading or watching an instructional video. Try building competence by establishing a new cultural norm that encourages people to dedicate weekly time to learning.

You might even consider doing what Elena did with her son: make time during a one-on-one meeting with staff members to discuss their values for learning. You might help reignite the fire of competence that was extinguished along the way to adulthood. You can also practice leadership skills proven to build competence, such as those described in the next section.

How to Build Competence

Building people's competence includes creating a work environment that promotes learning while helping people develop confidence in their abilities. Here are two specific leadership skills that help you deliver on that dual responsibility:

- Show and tell how to do a skill.
- Facilitate problem-solving.

Show and Tell How to Do a Skill

Your most demanding role may be developing people's ability and energy to achieve their goals. That means knowing how to set timelines, establish priorities, evaluate performance, define roles, and generate action plans. But the least-used leadership behavior may be one of the most essential: showing and telling how—or teaching people the skills necessary—to achieve their goals.[14] Don't ignore people's skill development or consider it inconsequential. Evidence for the quality of your leadership lies in whether the people you lead demonstrate progress in mastering the skills required for their success and meeting their everyday challenges and opportunities, or not.

Leaders who fail to show people how to achieve their outcomes have plenty of excuses. Maybe you've caught yourself impatiently thinking, "If I need to tell you how to do it, I might as well do it myself." Perhaps you're saddled with beliefs such as "I shouldn't have to tell him how to do it; that's what I hired him to do!" or "I don't have the time." A legitimate excuse for not showing and telling others how to do what they need to learn is that you don't know how to do it yourself. In that case, your responsibility is to ensure access to training resources.

But the biggest obstacle to showing and telling how to complete a task lies in your answer to this question: Are you a good teacher? You can be an expert at what you do and value learning and still not be a good teacher. Being good at what you do doesn't make you good at teaching others how to do it. For proof, consider sports heroes who made lousy coaches. What surprises me is that the reason cited for athletes not being good coaches is that they tend to be "insanely competitive, impatient, and difficult to work with."[15] That may be true. But let's be clear about the real reason.

People who excel in their field probably don't understand (or remember) the process they went through to learn it—let alone how to break it down for others to learn. An essential aspect of effective leadership is developing people and helping them improve their skill set. If you are one of those experts who doesn't know how to teach what you do, it's time you learned how to help others learn.

You will find some of the best examples for showing how to do something on the internet. YouTube instructional videos have taught me how to pop amaranth, connect my old Wii Fit to a new smart television, and repair the temperature gauge in my Keurig coffee maker. Showing and telling how requires that you provide the learner with an accurate description of the intended outcome and a demonstration of action steps for getting the desired results.

Try this: pick something you need to learn, search for instructional videos on YouTube, then compare the videos, noticing how the expert you gravitate toward—and are willing to watch over and over again until you master the skill—applies the fundamentals of showing and telling how.

Good online instructors plot out what they want you to learn and how you will learn it. They sequence action steps. Compare their approach to how some leaders delegate an outcome without taking the time to break it down into discrete actions that lead to the desired results—whether completing a budget, mastering a new software application, or following a sales procedure.

Take heed from Mr. Miyagi. I love using *The Karate Kid* as an example of telling and showing how. The way Mr. Miyagi develops Daniel's ability is masterful. He begins by deepening connection. "No such thing as bad student, only bad teacher. Teacher say, student do." Mr. Miyagi and Daniel-San make a teacher-student pact based on Daniel's profound desire to learn karate. But Mr. Miyagi also encourages choice by clarifying Daniel's options: follow Mr. Miyagi's teaching or walk away without knowing how to fight.

Despite moments of frustration, Mr. Miyagi encourages Daniel to trust him and the process. In the end, the instruction to "Wax on, wax off" results in Daniel-San's ability to block punches. But of course, because Mr. Miyagi continually deepened connection by providing a larger context of purpose and values, Daniel's learning journey was far more profound than learning a skill. A good teacher goes beyond building skills to instilling invaluable life lessons by encouraging choice, deepening connection, and, ultimately, building competence.

> A good teacher goes beyond building skills to instilling invaluable life lessons by encouraging choice, deepening connection, and, ultimately, building competence.

Facilitate Problem-Solving

Are you up for a little experiment? Ask one of your team members (or a colleague willing to play along) if he or she will help you solve a riddle. Your role is to facilitate your accomplice in finding a solution without imposing your own ideas. Here is the Two Jugs riddle: A man had a jug full of lemonade and a jug full of milk. He poured them into one large vat, yet he kept the lemonade separate from the milk. How?

Having led hundreds of leaders through this activity, we found they faced one of two challenges:

- When leaders didn't know the solution, they focused on solving the problem for themselves. They tended to forget that their job was to facilitate someone else's problem-solving.
- When leaders did know the answer, they tended to lead the witness, so to speak, and direct rather than guide the problem solver. Sometimes in their impatience, they just shared the solution.

If you think your job is to solve people's problems, think again. As a leader, your role is to teach people you lead how to solve their own problems. For people to become independent, self-reliant problem solvers, they must develop the confidence to solve problems and come to appropriate conclusions independently. That's the essence of building competence.

> **As a leader, your role is to teach people you lead how to solve their own problems.**

My husband and I were working to develop leadership skills with store managers for a major US retailer. One day, touring a store with its manager, we witnessed an awkward scene. A customer was loudly complaining about having to stand in line too long to make her purchase. The checkout clerk was obviously frustrated.

The manager was embarrassed. She admitted that her assistant manager, whose job is to schedule the sales associates, complained almost daily about not having enough staff to cover the checkout stands. She explained how she had tried to solve the problem, but being understaffed was a budget issue that neither she nor the assistant manager had any authority to change.

At a coaching session later that afternoon, we used the scenario to teach the manager how to facilitate problem-solving with the assistant manager. We outlined a simple method of exploring the problem by (1) using inquiry to understand the problem, (2) generating possible alternatives, (3) examining the consequences of those alternatives, (4) making a choice, and (5) evaluating the choice.

As the manager facilitated the assistant manager on the first step to clarify the problem, it became evident that both of them had accepted the problem as understaffing. Neither of them controlled the budget that allowed for hiring more staff members, so by accepting that definition of the problem, attempts at problem-solving had failed. We encouraged them to continue exploring the issue. Were there other ways of defining the problem?

Within moments, a different understanding of the problem emerged: ineffective scheduling during peak hours. The problem wasn't a lack of staff but how they were deployed. By clarifying the real issue, the problem of being understaffed that neither manager could control became a matter of reallocating resources, which the assistant store manager could control.

Both managers gained two powerful insights that day:

- Teaching someone how to solve problems is impossible if you don't have a model for problem-solving.
- The way to build competence and self-reliant problem solvers is to transparently and consistently facilitate their problem-solving instead of trying to solve their problems.

Facilitating the people you lead helps them see the power of their own ideas. Building competence means that you help people develop the confidence to effectively solve work-related problems on their own.

I hope you take on the challenge I posed at the beginning of this section. You have a choice of how you want to facilitate the Two Jugs riddle with a willing partner:

- You can facilitate finding the solution without knowing the answer yourself. Notice if you tend to get overly involved and abandon the problem-solving process, making it all about your experience, not the other person's.
- You can go to this endnote,[16] where the solution is revealed, then facilitate someone finding a solution you already know. In this case, notice if you try to manipulate or guide the person trying to solve the problem or, worse, get impatient and reveal the answer.

Either way, something fantastic can happen when you stick with the problem-solving process instead of overdirecting. The person you're facilitating comes up with a better or more creative solution than the "right answer." That's one of the wonders of facilitating problem-solving with others.

Ask Mindful Questions to Facilitate a Mojo Moment

One evening, my husband returned from a business trip to find me in a vortex of anxiety. I was madly trying to meet a product development deadline. As he entered my home office, I didn't even look up from my computer as I blurted out how hard I'd been working, the tremendous pressure I was under, and the stress I felt from people waiting for documents I hadn't completed yet.

After a long pause, I glanced up, thinking I better be sure it was Drea and not an intruder standing in the doorway. He smiled at me and gently and lovingly asked a question that shook me to my core: "Are you enjoying your work?"

My life flashed before me. I realized that I *was* enjoying my work—I'd chosen this path because it brought significance to my life, and I was good at it. But I also recognized that as much as I loved my work, I loved my husband more. I had chosen to partner with him to make meaning together and support one another's spiritual development. Suddenly, I was struck by my hypocrisy. Why was I complaining and stressed if I enjoyed my work so much? Why was I creating such negative and unwelcoming energy if I loved my husband?

To my surprise—and my husband's—I burst into tears. I did my best to explain the emotional response. I was shocked by the recognition of the person I was, not the person I longed to be. My husband listened empathetically, then offered a great solution: "Let's go out for Mexican food and a margarita." The dinner conversation was a turning point for me—and I don't credit the tequila.

Through his simple and nonjudgmental question, Drea had stimulated a mindful moment. My emotion stemmed from the obvious incongruence of my stated values with my behavior. I saw the truth and options for doing and being something different. I would have gotten defensive if he'd directly pointed out the gap between my values and actions.

Over dinner, I declared my intention not to impose my negative energy on Drea again. We will both attest that I became a different person that night. I shifted my motivational outlook regarding work from a suboptimal to an optimal outlook. Of course, I haven't been perfect! I can slip into the imposed motivational outlook when I'm physically tired or mindless. But thanks to that one mindful moment, I can access my values and purpose when I need to shift to an aligned, integrated, or inherent motivational outlook.

This anecdote occurred over a decade ago. Since that night, I have passionately pursued and tested mindful questions you can ask yourself to facilitate what I call a Mojo Moment. These questions have been refined over the past twelve years with leaders worldwide.

Mindful Questions That Encourage Choice

When it comes to people's goal or situation, ask them these questions:

- What choices have you made? How do you feel about those choices? Why?
- What choices do you have? What choices could you make going forward?
- Do you feel the goal or situation was imposed on you? Why?

Remember, sometimes reminding people they have a choice is all it takes for them to make one.

Mindful Questions That Deepen Connection

When it comes to people's goal or situation, ask them these questions:

- How might it give you a greater sense of belonging or genuine connection to others?
- How might it align with your values and purpose? Can you find meaning in it? Why?
- If you feel what is being asked of you is unjust, what would be fairer? Why?

Remember, a goal without meaning takes people nowhere meaningful.

Mindful Questions That Build Competence

When it comes to people's goal or situation, ask them these questions:

- What skills or experience do you have that might prove helpful?
- What have you learned? What new skills could you learn?
- What insights have you gained—or might gain—that could help you move forward?

Remember, when you limit growth opportunities, you also limit people's creativity, resilience, and ability to embrace change.

These questions are effective because they facilitate people's internal framing of choice, connection, and competence. Asking people to reflect on recent or potential decisions related to their goal or situation encourages choice. Asking people to consider how their goal or situation aligns with values, purpose, or meaning deepens connection. Asking people what they've learned—or could learn—from their goal or situation builds competence. Try asking these questions in your next goal-setting session, problem-solving discussion, coaching conversation, or one-to-one meeting.

Case in Point: Discovering What Works

A supervisor for a large construction company shared this story with me. I think it's a compelling case for applying your leadership capacity to encourage choice, deepen connection, and build competence.

The supervisor noticed that one of his employees was frequently late and appeared distracted. The supervisor admitted he wasn't good at having personal conversations with team members and that he knew little about the young man other than he was married and had two children.

Addressing the situation indirectly, the supervisor asked the young man how he and his family were managing the challenges of the pandemic, pointing out that remote learning was a struggle in his own home. The employee broke down. His wife was an emergency room nurse, he said. They had two kids in early elementary school and no family help. Trying to juggle schedules and work was taking its toll.

The supervisor called together his team and explained the situation. He encouraged the group to brainstorm alternatives. The supervisor told me he was "blown away" by the empathy and understanding demonstrated by the group. They collaborated on redesigning their workflow to provide a flexible schedule that allowed the young man time at home during critical times for his kids and in the office. Working together, the rest of the team shuffled their own schedules to make life easier for the struggling father.

The supervisor reported, "I learned that being empathetic and having a casual conversation with someone may be one of the greatest gifts I can give my people as a leader. But I also realized that as a leader, I have the power to give people choices. In this case, I trusted my team's competence enough to give them a choice on how to figure it out. The result is that the entire team felt they were doing something good. They chose to support the man's wife—a healthcare worker—and one of their own. They interpreted the changes as an opportunity for connection rather than an inconvenience."

The supervisor doesn't plan to return to normal as his team enters the new, more complex world of hybrid work. Instead, he wants to continue exploring opportunities to improve people's optimal motivation by encouraging choice, deepening connection, and building competence.

Recapping "If Motivating People Doesn't Work . . . What Does?"

Chapter 4 asks these questions: What changes would your organization experience if you resisted archaic and disproven leadership theories driving people in the wrong direction with unintended consequences? What might be different if you developed the leadership capacity to improve the quality of people's motivation?

Developing your leadership capacity to encourage choice, deepen connection, and build competence supports your leadership intention and effectiveness. The optimal motivation people experience through your motivational leadership is the path to workplace effectiveness and thriving.

5

Rethinking Leadership Now That Everything Else Has Changed

Change. You think we would be better at something that permeates every part of life, yet we struggle. People feel depleted from change. Leaders are exhausted. Dramatic changes keep them awake at night—managing a more sophisticated and awakened workforce that demands hybrid options, meaningful work, flexibility, equality, justice, and organizations that care about their well-being.

Do you wish you could wave a change wand and suddenly your workforce is achieving their goals and thriving simultaneously? I can't sell you a magic wand, but I can offer you a solution. You know firsthand what research proves: performance and motivation go hand in hand. Productivity suffers when leaders fail to create a culture that supports flourishing. The magic of the three leadership capacities introduced in chapter 4 is that when you encourage choice, deepen connection, and build competence, you also foster resilience, stimulate creativity, and promote well-being. Change is challenging but it doesn't have to be tormenting. Your leadership capacity can help people adapt to change, be highly productive, and not suffer so much in the process. Traditional leadership doesn't do that.

If there was ever a time to rethink how you lead, it's now. You have an unprecedented opportunity to take advantage of this clarion call to integrate motivation science into your leadership practice.

A New Leadership Imperative: Improving People's Psychological Sense

Imagine you're at a conference, and the speaker engages the group in an activity. Along with your fellow participants, you comply. You stand up and find a partner—someone you've never met before. Then you do as instructed: you and the stranger wordlessly stare at each other for sixty seconds. Finally, the minute is up, and you turn back to back. You have one minute to change five things about your appearance. You take off your watch and stash it in your pocket. You remove your jacket. You shift your glasses from your eyes to the top of your head. You slip off a shoe. You and your partner turn to face each other and identify the changes. You each do a decent job of noticing what's different.

You think the activity is finished, so you begin to rearrange yourself. But the facilitator instructs you to turn back-to-back again and change five more things about your appearance!

You groan but obey. You switch your right and left shoes after removing one of your socks. You roll up a pant leg. You take off your wedding ring and stash it with the watch in your pocket. Now you're at a loss. You don't have any more jewelry or clothing to remove. You and your partner turn to face each other again and identify the changes, finding it a bit more challenging than the last round.

Irritated, you begin to put yourself back together. But you can't believe your ears—the facilitator tells you to turn back-to-back and change ten more things about your appearance! Although a few people are shamelessly having a blast—one woman seems to have turned herself inside out, and one guy is shirtless—you are with the majority who rebels and refuses to continue.

I've conducted this activity for small groups of twenty and in ballrooms filled with over a thousand people. Still, the outcome is predictable. When I reveal the following statements describing how people typically react when told to change, I get laughs from people who recognize themselves:

- You feel awkward, even silly, at the beginning of the change effort.
- You focus on what you will have to give up, not gain.
- You feel you are facing change alone, even though others are going through the same activity.
- You can handle only so much change but notice some people have a greater tolerance than you do.
- You fear no one will notice the changes you make or appreciate your efforts at change.

- You are concerned that you don't have enough resources to make more changes.
- When the pressure is off, you can't wait to revert to "normal."

I've often heard that people don't resist change; after all, a baby cries because she *wants* a change. People's negative reaction isn't to change but to their perceived loss of control. I believe that's true—but it's only one-third of the explanation. People also resist change without meaning or an opportunity for growth.

During the change activity's debrief, most people realized the cause of their angst: suboptimal motivation. They felt participating in the activity was imposed—they didn't feel in control or free to sit it out, which eroded their psychological need for choice. They didn't regard the activity as meaningful or as having a clear purpose. They wanted to shut down from embarrassment and vulnerability, which thwarted their psychological need for connection. And they were frustrated—they couldn't handle the demand to make ten changes, let alone another ten, which undermined their psychological need for competence.

But another aha moment comes with three more revelations:

- What if you had created choice by interpreting the activity as an opportunity instead of an imposition?
- What if you had created connection by acknowledging your vulnerability and taking advantage of the available resources in the room by borrowing someone else's sweater, scarf, or tie?

- What if you had created competence by tapping into your curiosity and embracing a growth mindset?

By fulfilling the psychological needs for choice, connection, and competence, the participants could have made changes to their appearance all day long!

People come to an inevitable conclusion: the quality of their motivation determines their ability—or inability—to tolerate change, discover creative solutions, and experience resilience in the face of challenging demands. The type of motivation they had for the activity either drained their energy or generated vitality.

This change activity helps explain how moments of change can be taxing for everyone involved. Coping and thriving through change requires complex processing, reflection, and learning—and optimal motivation. Faced with mandated and ever-growing demands for change these days, leaders and followers alike must skillfully use their *psychological sense* to navigate difficult times successfully.

Psychological sense is a person's emotional and cognitive ability to fulfill psychological needs and experience optimal motivation, a state of thriving, and sustained high performance.

> Psychological sense is a person's emotional and cognitive ability to fulfill psychological needs and experience optimal motivation, a state of thriving, and sustained high performance.

How Your Leadership Can Improve People's Psychological Sense

Now that everything has changed, we need a workforce of self leaders who accept responsibility and take the initiative to gain the mindset and the skill set for success in their role. I'm a big believer in self leadership. That means individuals at all levels need to develop and improve their psychological sense—the ability to fulfill their need for choice, connection, and competence. With improved psychological sense, they can make changes all day, if that's what's required.

I'm also an advocate for leadership that doesn't block people's natural inclination to experience optimal motivation. The quality of your leadership can help transform psychological sense into common sense.

When you encourage choice, deepen connection, and build competence through your everyday leadership efforts, you are facilitating people's ability to experience optimal motivation. We know that the more optimal motivation people experience, the more they want. It's a virtuous cycle: you promote choice, connection, and competence so people can develop and improve their psychological sense; they experience optimal motivation and improve their ability to navigate the complexities of change, strengthen effective coping mechanisms, and thrive despite the changes they face.

This chapter challenges you to rethink how you've approached leadership in the past to meet the needs of a workplace that has radically changed and requires psychological sense to evolve.

Rethink the Great (Fill in the Blank)

During the height of the postpandemic Great Disruption (also called the Great Resignation, among other names), this headline caught my attention: "The Great Resignation Turns to the Great Regret as Worker Needs Are Not Being Met, Expert Says."[1]

Suddenly venerable business sites were reporting on the Great Regret and its cousin, the quiet quitting, or quitting in place. McKinsey & Company claimed the Great Attrition had become the Great Renegotiation.[2] But no matter how many trendy names we assign to the phenomenon of workers changing jobs, it's worth exploring.

We won't know for years how permanent the postpandemic changes will be. But right now, I think companies, leaders, and the great resigners themselves need an empirically based explanation of the story behind what happened. More importantly, we all need to understand how to effectively write our own end story by applying reality-based solutions.

The Story behind the Story

During the Great Whatever-You-Call-It, millions of people quit or changed jobs for myriad reasons. But a comprehensive study by McKinsey & Company revealed the major motivations behind people seeking a new employer:

- Gaining autonomy and flexibility
- Escaping a toxic culture and the feeling of not being appreciated, and craving a company culture focused on

employee health and well-being that emphasizes meaning and purpose
- Having access to opportunities for growth and learning,
career development, and opportunities for advancement[3]

Notice a pattern? These people are not lazy or looking for a
handout. They are dissatisfied employees seeking choice, connection, and competence.

People leave jobs that thwart their psychological needs. But
without an understanding of motivation, they are not likely to
find a job that fulfills them. Misinterpreting their dissatisfaction as unhappiness, many job seekers fell prey to the cultural
trap of external motivation. Enticed by the usual suspects of
money, status, and the grass-is-always-greener syndrome, the
déjà vu of unfulfilled needs leads to their Great Regret. Let's
call it the Great Misunderstanding.

Rewriting the Story of the Great Misunderstanding

Disgruntled employees need your leadership to facilitate their
psychological sense and avoid a great misunderstanding. Consider how your leadership capacity can help them shift their
motivational outlook when it comes to the top three reasons
they cite for leaving their job.

Autonomy, Flexibility, Control, and Choice

Ironically, the restrictions on staying home during the pandemic years helped people appreciate autonomy. They reveled

in newly found discretionary time gained from throwing on a pair of sweatpants instead of donning a suit, walking to the next room instead of commuting to and from the office, raiding their fridge when hungry instead of being forced to eat at an expected hour, and having grace time to decompress at the end of the day instead of being stuck in traffic.

The flexibility people experienced while working from home was in stark contrast to laboring in a command-and-control workplace perceived as toxic and uncaring with few opportunities to grow and learn. Is it any wonder people wanted to escape? With studies revealing that productivity didn't suffer from people working at home, the workforce put organizations on notice: they want continued autonomy, flexibility, control, and choice.

Remember, if you want to help improve people's psychological sense, sharpen your leadership capacity to encourage choice: explore options within boundaries, present goals and timelines as valuable information, and refrain from using controlling language. Focus on establishing a work environment— no matter its location—where people don't feel manipulated by power, incentives to drive results, and the pressure to perform.

Meaning, Well-Being, Justice, and Connection

Teaching people the skill of motivation is an effective strategy for developing people's psychological sense. When people know how to create choice, connection, and competence for themselves, they are more likely to experience meaningful work.[4] Zaid Khan illustrates my point in his viral video describing his rationale for quiet quitting.[5]

It saddens me that Khan and thousands of workers are choosing to quit but stay in their jobs. They are undermining the organization, its employees, and its customers. But the poignant point is that they are hurting themselves most of all.

Khan believes that by not engaging, he's reducing his stress. But with over half of his life connected to work, Khan's opportunity loss from quiet quitting is heartrending. Many of the quiet quitters and great resigners either silently or explicitly yearn for meaningful work. What they probably don't understand is that meaning is a by-product of fulfilling their psychological needs.

Many of us have learned the hard way that no job or workplace is perfect. Obstacles, challenges, bad bosses, grumpy coworkers, and some boring tasks are facts of life. But with the skill of motivation, instead of bemoaning a workplace rife with pressure and devoid of meaning, the quiet quitters can learn to shift their motivation and experience optimal motivation anytime and anywhere they choose. By creating choice, connection, and competence themselves, they can flourish no matter where they are—at work or play.

People who don't develop the psychological sense to experience optimal motivation in their job eventually discover that all the perks in the world still lead to meaningless work.

> **People who don't develop the psychological sense to experience optimal motivation in their job eventually discover that all the perks in the world still lead to meaningless work.**

Despite claiming to be motivated by meaningful work, too many people find themselves in unsatisfying jobs because money was the reason they accepted the job. Pursuing money to compensate for lack of choice, connection, and competence may promise a fatter pocketbook. But we know the pursuit of money as a primary end goal almost always hinders well-being and depletes the positive energy needed to sustain the increase in income.

Money is symbolic. Yes, people need a living wage—but not just for survival. People need to feel a sense of belonging and genuine relationships to thrive. So when Adam Grant proposed extending raises to veteran workers to keep them happily in place, it wasn't what was being done that mattered but how and why.[6] Instead of positioning increased pay as an incentive or reward for staying—or as a bribe to endure undue pressure to perform—higher wages need to be positioned as a genuine demonstration of gratitude that deepens connection.

Desiring more money isn't always a sign of suboptimal motivation though. When people ask for more money because their wages are unfair, they could be optimally motivated to advocate for justice. Equity—or lack of it—is an issue that erodes connection in the workplace. A common myth is that people don't leave companies, they leave bad bosses. The truth is just the opposite. People leave companies that enable that bad boss to exist. Injustice is the primary reason people leave organizations, and money is often symbolic of workplace inequity. The bottom line is people cannot experience connection in an unfair organization.

Learning, Growth, Progress, and Competence

Imagine a skier who never progresses past the bunny slope or an entrepreneur who never manages to develop people to expand the business. The reason so many of us quit before we really get started is that our progress is stifled. Think about a goal you chose to pursue because you found it meaningful, but you ended up quitting. What happened? You may have become discouraged because the goal was harder than you thought it would be, and you didn't have the time required to learn. Maybe you lacked the resources and training you needed. In the end, your progress wasn't satisfying. Despite your psychological need for choice and connection being fulfilled, your competence was thwarted.

We give lip service to creating learning organizations, but as a leader, if you don't proactively promote time and resources to training and development, people will leave. The baby boomer generation and the generations before them focused on staying in one company as long as possible. I remember when you were chastised for showing too many job changes on a résumé. Today's generation will have five times the number of jobs their parents did. Their currency is not longevity but marketable skills. One way to hold on to younger workers is by providing opportunities for them to become proficient in a variety of tasks, jobs, and skills. The irony is that the more marketable you help them become, the more likely they are to remain loyal.

You can rewrite the story of the Great Misunderstanding through your leadership capacity. You can prevent people's psychological needs from being thwarted so they are less likely to pursue greener pastures. You can facilitate their psychological sense by encouraging choice, deepening connection, and building competence to help them thrive where they are, avoiding great regret.

> We give lip service to creating learning organizations, but as a leader, if you don't proactively promote time and resources to training and development, people will leave.

Rethink Where and How People Work

We all want to see the trauma and discontent revealed during the pandemic experience in our rearview mirror. But these problems will persist if people aren't optimally motivated wherever they work—in the office, at home, or on the road. The real head-scratcher for executives seems to be managing a hybrid workplace. Take these four statements from CEOs announcing their company's hybrid work policy. I hope you can spot the statement that has the best chance of improving people's psychological sense and generating optimal motivation.

- "Only the least engaged people want to work from home." (Sandeep Mathrani, CEO, WeWork)

  The pushback was swift against the WeWork CEO's bold claim that only the "least engaged" people want to continue working from home.[7] Mathrani had an ulterior motive for people not to work from home and rent office space from WeWork—which he acknowledged in an apology. How effective do you think Mathrani's leadership is at encouraging choice, deepening connection, and building competence? Is his approach better or worse than Elon Musk's?

- "Remote work is no longer acceptable. Anyone who wishes to do remote work must be in the office for a minimum of 40 hours a week. If you don't show up, we will assume you have resigned." (Elon Musk, CEO, Tesla, SpaceX, and Twitter)

    The backlash was just as severe against Musk after he made this announcement in 2022.[8] He also appeared to have an agenda behind the statement: Musk needed to reduce his workforce and thought this approach might help eliminate people without having to pay severance. Compare Musk's statement with the approach taken by Chris Wollerman.

- "We ask all team members to work in the office at least twice a week. To ensure you don't walk into a ghost town, we surveyed which two days of the week you preferred, and the majority voted for Tuesdays and Thursdays. The primary reasons for needing you in the office twice a week are to build community in a way that only in-person interaction can achieve, welcome our new hires (over 80 in the past year), and show a united front to our clients on virtual and face-to-face meetings. To take advantage of the time you're here, we'll schedule training sessions for skills that are best learned in person. We'll also sponsor company social events you can choose to attend if you're in the mood for some fun." (Chris Wollerman, CEO, InnovaSystems)

When Wollerman made this announcement to more than three hundred employees, he had an agenda too.[9] He believes in creating a workplace where optimal motivation is the norm. He even built a motivation wizard into its proprietary Inspire Software for people to identify their motivational outlook on a goal and discuss it during one-on-one meetings. The result? As the average retention rate for US companies dropped dramatically during the pandemic years, InnovaSystems enjoyed low attrition—and a retention rate over 25 percent higher than the national average.

- "Until we figure out our hybrid work strategy, you can either work at home or come to the office."

  In poll results from webinars I conducted, most companies handled the hybrid work issue this way. Leadership appears woefully underprepared, especially considering that a McKinsey & Company survey reports that nine of ten organizations are combining remote, hybrid, and on-site working. Without clarity on handling this extreme change in the workplace, the entire workforce is experiencing anxiety.[10]

Regardless of your preference for where and how people work, the issue presents an opportunity to apply your leadership capacities to encourage choice, deepen connection, and build competence. The following ideas will help improve people's psychological sense, paving the way for positive results like InnovaSystems experienced.

Encourage Choice

Remember that encouraging choice doesn't mean giving people the freedom to choose any alternative—it means providing options within boundaries. It's essential to take the time to discuss the nature of different jobs and the roles' requirements. If you can offer some people a choice to work from home, on-site, or in a hybrid model, be transparent that not everyone will have the same options. Treating people with equality doesn't necessarily mean they all get the same deal—it means they get the same level of respect and consideration. Procedural justice is essential when encouraging choice in a workforce where one size doesn't fit all.

Deepen Connection

An intriguing trend is the traditional persona of the CEO morphing into the chief empathy officer. Revealing vulnerability, implementing health and wellness plans, and demonstrating empathy are essential leadership practices for deepening connection with people, whether they are working on-site, at home, remotely, or on a hybrid schedule. The most optimally motivated people make choices that align with meaningful values and contribute to the greater good. Help people explore options and make choices that suit their role, fulfill their family values, support coworkers (and enable coworkers to support them), and best serve customers, clients, and stakeholders.

Build Competence

Determine the feasibility, level of technical skills required, and equipment necessary to be in a hybrid work environment. Be honest if you can't afford to duplicate the resources—access to those resources may be a good rationale for coming to the office a few days per week. Agree to measures of competence and progress. Set high-quality SMART (specific, motivating, attainable, relevant, and time-bound) goals that reflect the outcomes for the role. Monitor progress and adjust accordingly. Regularly ask people to share what they're learning from wherever they are learning it.

The beauty of recreating our workplaces by creating choice, connection, and competence is that when people thrive, they also produce results—wherever they work.

Rethink Goal Setting

The quality of a goal matters. Even a well-constructed goal will fail to improve performance if it's not optimally motivating to the person pursuing it. That's why I changed the *M* in the SMART goal-setting acronym from *measurable* to *motivating*.[11]

But remember, not all motivation is created equal. To rethink goal setting now that everything else has changed, you need to appreciate the difference between low-quality goals that drive suboptimal motivation and high-quality goals that promote optimal motivation.

> To rethink goal setting now that everything else has changed, you need to appreciate the difference between low-quality goals that drive suboptimal motivation and high-quality goals that promote optimal motivation.

Patricia managed over a dozen hair stylists in a busy salon. She embarked on a goal-setting initiative that promoted entrepreneurial behaviors to increase the salon's income and profitability.

Believing in the importance of servant leadership, she took the time to explore each stylist's hopes for the future and help them turn those dreams into SMART goals. For example, one woman wanted a bigger home, so her goal became "Double the tips I receive over the next three months." A young man was excited by being a celebrity stylist, so he set a goal to "recruit one celebrity client over the next six months and promote my achievement through social media."

The problem? Despite appearing to be SMART, their goals were at risk of being low quality. The quality of the woman's goal to double her tips so she could buy a bigger home depends on her motivation for desiring a larger house. If she needed more space based on her value for improving the quality of life for her family, the goal might be considered high quality. But if she craves the status and enhanced image the home promises, her goal would be low quality.

Being a celebrity stylist appears to be a low-quality goal based on external motivation. The question is why the young man wants to be a celebrity stylist. If it's to be more popular, famous, or admired by others, then it's low quality. But maybe the goal reflects a way for the young man to objectively measure his creativity, innovation, and excellence. Then it might be considered high quality. Still, an objective, inspiring, and higher-quality goal might be to attract three new clients who return monthly over the next six months, trusting that satisfying his clientele could lead to his dream of being a celebrity stylist.

The lesson from Patricia is that without facilitating a deeper exploration of the motivation behind the goals, she potentially set them up for suboptimal motivation. They might experience short-term gains but will not be able to sustain the positive energy required for succeeding in the long run. Externally based goals tend to generate pressure, tension, stress, and guilt that diminish the goal setter's well-being and negatively affect the quality of work and level of customer service.

To prevent people from setting low-quality goals, avoid goals measured by any of the following:

- Social recognition, such as increasing Facebook friends or LinkedIn contacts, to improve personal or professional status
- Image and appearance, such as losing weight to look good at a reunion or be more attractive to others
- Material success, such as earning more money to impress others, buy a flashy car, or move to a prestigious neighborhood to enhance status or gain power
- Winning, such as when the purpose is to best someone else to elevate yourself, gain a reward, or avoid the perceived stigma of losing

Research shows that even if people achieve low-quality goals, they don't experience the vitality and positive effects of high-quality goals. They rarely sustain or repeat their high-performing ways. Worse, goals that generate suboptimal motivation are more likely to lead to depression and unhealthy physical symptoms.[12]

Suboptimal Motivation Undermines Optimal Motivation

Another hazard of low-quality goals is that the suboptimal motivation they generate undermines optimal motivation. For example, let's say you're motivated to win the sales trip to the Bahamas and still provide the best quality service to your customer. You cannot be suboptimally motivated and optimally motivated at the same time—motivation is not additive. Of course, suboptimal motivation plus suboptimal motivation equals suboptimal motivation. But—and this is an important *but*—suboptimal motivation plus *optimal* motivation still equals suboptimal motivation. When push comes to shove, you'll do what it takes to get to the Bahamas because suboptimal motivation tends to extinguish optimal motivation.[13]

The same scenario occurs with goals based on imposed motivation, such as fear, threats, revenge, or anger (even if it's self-righteous anger). Optimal motivation is a powerful state, but regretfully, it can be diverted by low-quality goals that focus on the shiny objects of external motivation or the burden of imposed motivation.[14]

Low-Quality Goals Are Deceptive

You might wonder, Isn't it good to be driven to excel, raise the trophy, or be declared a champion? Isn't it normal to want popularity, status, and power? The Golden State Warriors basketball organization provides an exemplary example of the empirically proven answer to these questions. Team members, the coaching staff, and owners understand that setting records, winning championships, and gaining fame and fortune are by-products of setting high-quality goals based on excellence, continuous improvement, and teamwork.

Even if you're not a basketball fan, please watch the terrific post-finals interview of Stephen Curry by ESPN's Malika Andrews.[15] Viewers get a profound insight into Curry's motivation when she asks him if the individual most valuable player (MVP) award was something he'd wanted. He replied, "Of course." But he revealed his true motivation in his next breath: "Jerry West is the only player to win the MVP without his team winning the finals, so me winning the MVP would mean that we won the whole thing."

To Curry, winning the finals MVP was symbolic of something more meaningful to him—the team's win. Watch his reaction as he's awarded the MVP trophy, and you understand why his teammates describe him as selfless, the ultimate team player, and a humble superstar. I believe his optimal motivation is fueled by how he cherishes his team, fans, and community over his ego and need for status.

Stephen Curry epitomizes what the research cited in this book tells us about competition: winning can be optimally motivating if the pressure to win—for whatever reason—is not the primary motivation. The downsides of competition are that the pressure to win and the fear of losing erode choice, connection, and competence. An upside of competition is that it can bestow abundant opportunities for connecting with teammates and providing the feedback and information that lead to mastery.

The Warriors epitomize a team with psychological sense. You can see the results of setting high-quality goals through the joy, exhilaration, and success generated by their optimal motivation.

You can facilitate your team members' high-quality goals by promoting goals that focus on the following areas:

- Personal growth, such as improving listening skills or practicing mindfulness
- Affiliation, such as forming a mentoring relationship or participating in a worthwhile organization
- Community, such as advocating for a policy that promotes workplace justice or contributes to the welfare of others
- Physical health, such as increasing strength or lowering blood pressure
- Improving one's financial situation for the right reasons, such as saving for retirement or supporting a child's education
- Growth and learning, such as mastering a new skill, gaining expertise on a topic, or demonstrating proficiency in a chosen area
- Competition framed as informational rather than controlling

Motivation Is the Soul of the Goal

You may need your team members to achieve mundane goals, such as the directive to submit 95 percent of their project reports by the deadline during the third quarter. While this goal meets most of the SMART goal requirements, you need a motivational outlook conversation to determine whether the goal is optimally motivating to the people pursuing it. The discussion should explore if the goal fulfills their psychological need for choice (they don't feel it's being imposed on them), connection (they can align the goal to meaningful values or a sense of purpose), and competence (they feel good about the skills they bring to it or are interested in the skills they'll gain from pursuing the goal).

What people yearn for in their work cannot be bought or achieved through low-quality goals pursued with suboptimal motivation. By rethinking your goal-setting approach, a high-quality goal combined with a motivational outlook conversation can be a profound and sustainable mechanism to promote people's well-being, sustained high performance, and improved psychological sense.

Rethink Feedback

Your feedback is always motivating, but not necessarily as you intend. Over 70 percent of people receiving feedback from their boss report it does as much harm as good—talk about suboptimal motivation![16]

I'm not suggesting you stop giving feedback. But I recommend rethinking the way you deliver it. We can provide the information people need to progress toward their goals while also improving their psychological sense. When you engage the three leadership capacities to deliver feedback, you almost ensure an optimally motivating experience for the person receiving the feedback—and you, the person giving it!

Deliver Feedback That Encourages Choice

Winston Churchill famously quipped that he was always ready to learn but didn't always like being taught. He's not alone. Think about the last time you gave someone feedback. Were they ready to learn but not open to being taught by you at that moment? Delivering feedback when someone isn't ready is a great way to erode autonomy. Their coping mechanism for combating their perceived loss of control might be to get defensive or belligerent or, the opposite, to passively shut down. They may dismiss the information, place blame, or resent you for being the messenger of bad news.

Instead of leading people to dread feedback, try these three practices that encourage choice so everyone can appreciate the upside of feedback:

- *Flip the feedback*—Establish a new norm where people regularly solicit your input rather than waiting for you to initiate giving feedback. When you conduct one-on-one meetings, set aside time for your team member to ask for feedback on critical goals and activities. Research indicates that when people ask for feedback, their psychological need for choice enables them to be more open and receptive to what they need to hear.
- *Ask for permission to provide feedback*—First, ask people if you can give them feedback. Then, provide a context and rationale for why you're giving it. For example, you can say, "You have expressed an interest in becoming a better team leader. I observed how you opened the meeting yesterday and noticed two techniques

you used to ease the tension in the room. I think you should consider using them in the future. I also have one insight to make the next meeting even more effective. Would you be open to hearing the feedback, or is there a better time?"

- *Be direct using autonomy-supportive language*—If you can't afford to wait or risk someone rejecting your offer of feedback, then deliver your message directly using autonomy-supportive language. For example, you can say, "I need to bring a matter to your attention, hear your perspective, and explore options. I received a complaint about how a customer service issue was handled. Let me give you the feedback directly, then let's discuss the situation from your perspective, lessons learned, and opportunities for reconciliation."[17]

Deliver Feedback That Deepens Connection

Personalized feedback includes evaluative phrases based on your personal opinion, including any of the following phrases:

- I am so proud of you.
- You make me happy when . . .
- You are amazing (wonderful, terrific, the bomb).
- I don't know what I'd do without you.
- You sure didn't disappoint me when you . . .
- I'm surprised at your failure to . . .
- You disappointed me when . . .
- I am so disappointed that you . . .
- I wish you had . . .

The irony of personalized feedback, including praise, is that it thwarts connection. This is especially true when you're in a one-up position of power as a leader, teacher, or parent responsible for developing someone's skill and commitment. Consider two examples of personalized feedback—information steeped with your judgment. Both are risky.

- "Sara, I am disappointed in you for being late with this report. It made life difficult not just for me but for others too. I need you to get these reports in on time in the future."

  Your disappointment in Sara may prompt her to change her behavior in the future but for the wrong reason—to avoid guilt, shame, or fear of not meeting your expectations. Pointing out Sara's unacceptable behavior by cloaking it in your disappointment can result in an imposed motivational outlook. Motivation science has shown that people working from this sub-optimal outlook to avoid feelings of guilt, shame, or fear are more prone to emotional and physical stress—and as a result are less creative in the short term and less productive in the long term.

- "Sara, I am proud of you for getting this report done ahead of time. It makes my life so much easier. I hope you can continue to be on time with deadlines in the future."

  Here, your praise for Sara risks her accepting the feedback for the wrong reason—to please you. Neuroscience demonstrates how praising stimulates the brain's reward center. Motivation science has documented the undermining effect of tangible rewards on productivity, creativity, innovation, and sustained effort. Intangible rewards, such as praise, tie to people's need for status, power, and image with the same eroding effect.

Remember why you provide feedback in the first place: to develop an individual's ability and positive energy to pursue a meaningful goal. Personalized feedback puts that outcome at risk. Personalized feedback draws on Sara's desire to please you or her need to avoid feelings of guilt, shame, or fear generated from your disapproval. Either way, she depends on you and your opinion rather than her own evaluation and ability to self-correct.

A problem lies with praise. My plea to avoid praising has been met with disagreement and even some personalized expressions of derision. But my experiences and the research are too compelling for me to ignore. Praising often results in conditional regard—meaning that a person's self-esteem, confidence, and self-worth are contingent on the opinion of leaders, teachers, and parents.

Children are especially susceptible to the downside of praise—interpreting the parent's praise as an expression of love. They believe their parent's love is contingent on their behavior and success, which leads to all kinds of aberrant behavior to please and impress. Both children and adults tend to resent the praiser, feeling controlled by the compliments and manipulated by the adulation. Self-Determination Theory research finds that giving praise risks eroding people's psychological needs for choice, connection, and competence.[17]

Carol Dweck's research reinforces how praise affects people's competence. She writes that praising intelligence and talent

erodes children's growth mindset: "Yes, children love praise. . . .
It really does give them a boost, a special glow—but only for the
moment. The minute they hit a snag, their confidence goes out
the window, and their motivation hits rock bottom. . . . If parents
want to give their children a gift, the best thing they can do is
teach their children to love challenges, be intrigued by mistakes,
enjoy effort, and keep on learning. That way, their children don't
have to be slaves of praise." Dweck warns that children raised
on praise are now in the workforce demanding tokens, stickers,
prizes, and praise for their every move.[18]

For the record, I want to acknowledge how hard it is to
refrain from praising. It makes us feel good, and we think it makes
the people we're praising feel good. But we have better ways to
deepen connection, such as helping them set high-quality and
meaningful goals. I urge you to remember this the next time
you have the urge to praise: the feedback you give says as much
about you as it does the person receiving it—maybe more.

Deliver Feedback That Builds Competence

Pure feedback is the antidote to personalized feedback. You can
wean people from their desire for your approval by providing them
with the information they need when they need it. Pure informational feedback offers the raw material for people to self-evaluate,
self-correct, and develop independence and resilience.

Pure informational feedback is nonjudgmental, descrip-
tive information about past performance or current behavior
that enables improvement. This could look like either one of
these:

- "Sara, your goal is to submit monthly reports on or before the fifteenth of the following month. This past quarter, you delivered all three reports well before the deadline. How do you feel about the goal and your performance?"

  This information allows Sara to interpret the feedback for herself. She is likely to internalize it as positive—mainly because there is agreement on her goal and expectations are clear.

- "Sara, your goal is to submit monthly reports on or before the fifteenth of the following month. This past quarter, you delivered two of three reports after the deadline. The one delivered before the deadline was missing a signature, so it needed to be resubmitted. The two submitted after the deadline met all the expected criteria. How do you feel about your efforts and progress toward your goal?"

  Notice that this pure informational feedback is designed to get Sara to think about her behavior and come to her own conclusions. The goal is stated; outcomes and expectations are clear. With pure informational feedback, Sara is less likely to expend emotional energy to deal with your judgment and more likely to explore her own motivation. Depending on Sara's level of development and need for training, the conversation could lead to a productive problem-solving conversation where you consider alternatives and partner on the steps Sara can take to adapt her future behavior.

Feedback Can Facilitate Psychological Sense

Personalized and judgmental feedback can land with a thud, shutting people down or provoking defensiveness. Personalized feedback is the junk food of motivation because the impetus for people's behavior comes from an external source: your approval or disapproval. On the other hand, pure informational feedback given in the context of an agreed-upon goal facilitates people's psychological sense so they choose to open up, accept your intentions as helpful, and learn from the information you provide. Pure feedback provides people with a healthy alternative: the information they need to change, improve, or maintain their behavior with a sense of choice, connection, and competence.

Rethink Tokens and Badges

I'm enthralled with a headband that measures five different brain waves while meditating, giving me real-time biofeedback. I listen to a raging storm through the accompanying app on my smartphone. The deeper I go into meditation, the calmer the wind gusts and pelting rain become. After about twenty minutes, I know I've gotten into a meditative state when, in the silence, I hear birds chirping. Amazing, right?

After a session, I check my analytics to see how often I lost focus and how long it took to regain it. I can see my progress from session to session, which is great. But you know what else I found? Tokens! I earned tokens by creating nine chirping birds. I meditated for two hours this week and got more tokens, which earned me a badge I can share on social media. It didn't take long before I noticed feeling pressured to make the birds chirp—which ironically elevated the storm's ferocity.

As much as I revel in the technology, I'm insulted by the company's belief that I need to be incentivized and rewarded for doing what I bought the product to help me do: develop mindfulness through meditation.

What is more antithetical to developing mindfulness than feeling the pressure to hear birds chirp so I can earn tokens, then setting up the potential for judgment by sharing my results on social media? To experience optimal motivation, I need to consciously ignore the pressure to make the birds chirp and remember that tokens can't buy me mindfulness.

To my chagrin, one of the biggest trends in the past ten years has been awarding tokens and badges in the workplace. Like it or not, tokenism is not going away soon. But before I succumb to the inevitability of tokens infiltrating every level of our work life, I plead with you to consider the potential consequences and downside of token mania.

If you've thrown tokens at a situation or are about to, will you take a moment to answer the ultimate question: *why*? If your answer falls into one of these three categories—fear, laziness, or misunderstanding—perhaps you'll rethink the token and try an alternative approach.

Avoid Rewarding Tokens Based on Your Fear

For almost two years, a CEO sent a detailed and heartfelt letter weekly to the entire organization sharing economic updates, revealing strategic decisions and their rationale, and describing his concerns and optimism about the company's future. People appreciated the quality of the information, but around the proverbial watercooler, they also gushed about his transparency, sensitivity, and vulnerability.

Then, one day, he suddenly announced that instead of sending his letter via email, he would post it on the company's internal site and reward people with tokens for reading it. I asked him why he felt he needed to offer an external reward for something people had been optimally motivated to do. His answer: "People like tokens."

In probing a bit more, I sensed he was afraid people would lose interest, and he'd lose the accolades along with their interest. He was betting that the incentives would allay his fears. But what if he'd asked people to reflect on how his posts influenced their relationship with the company? What if he asked people what value they found in the information he provided? What if he'd tapped into people's optimal motivation instead of depending on suboptimal motivation to get the behavior he wanted from people?

I've heard the counterargument that the incentives must work if people are doing what you ask them to do to earn the tokens. But how do you answer these questions: Now that people earn tokens for doing what you want them to do (e.g., reading the CEO's weekly letter), are they doing it with intent and interest? Or are they pretending to do it so they can earn tokens?

Research proves that the answer to the first question is often no; the answer to the second question is often yes. If you're rewarding tokens for fear of what might happen if you don't, I urge you to resist. Don't allow your fear to interfere with your leadership imperative to develop and improve people's psychological sense.

Take actions to mitigate your anxiety by helping people explore how doing what you are asking them to do might fulfill their need for choice, connection, and competence. In the end, why settle for compliance when you can foster the engagement and energy that comes from optimal motivation?

Avoid Basing Tokens on Your Laziness

The man I sat next to at a conference described his company's token-earning approach that incentivized people to complete training sessions. I asked him why he felt the need to reward people for learning. He explained that the information was inherently dull. He thought tokens would make the pain more bearable. In other words, tokens were easier than finding a way to make the training relevant and compelling.

Before defaulting to incentives for motivating people to do something boring, routine, or meaningless, ask why. If what you're asking people to do isn't worth investing your time to make it a worthwhile experience, maybe everyone's wasting their time. But if you conclude that encouraging people to do what you're asking of them is essential to their well-being, then don't take the lazy way out. Bribing people to engage in your project diminishes the quality of your project, but it also deprives them of discovering a worthwhile reason to engage. Don't let your laziness destroy an experience that could improve people's psychological sense.

Avoid Basing Tokens on
Misunderstanding Motivation

If you believe the best way to motivate people to learn, contribute, or work hard toward a common goal is to incentivize or reward them with tokens, maybe it's time to investigate your beliefs about human motivation. People enjoy learning. They want to contribute. They are willing to go through hell and back if they find meaning and purpose in the process. You may discover that people equipped with psychological sense want to succeed even more than you want them to.

Rethink Gamification

A high-level manager from a Fortune 500 company created a game based on one of my motivation books and reached out for feedback. I love games and wanted to support her efforts. But we ran into an early roadblock when I asked her the game's purpose. She stated her intention: she wanted to teach people about their psychological needs in a fun way. Her response was spot on. But the problem was she had designed the game with a different reason for playing: to win. Ironically, her gamification that intended to teach the skill of motivation undermined the very thing she was hoping people would learn: alternatives to suboptimal motivation.

It comes as no surprise that "gamification" is a growing phenomenon in organizations.[19] Sales groups started the trend based on the belief that most salespeople are motivated by money, trips, and winning. Then, ironically, HR departments embraced gamification to improve their employees' health and well-being. Now gaming is endorsed by organizations to facilitate education and effective performance.

To help explain why so many well-meaning managers get gamification wrong, I turned to Dr. Edward Deci and Dr. Richard Ryan, the fathers of Self-Determination Theory. They are arguably the most prominent motivation researchers in the world. Along with Dr. Scott Rigby, they are also cofounders of Immersyve and dedicated to studying and applying motivation science to gaming—including video games and the gamification of education.

How did these lauded researchers get involved in video gaming? For starters, if you don't play some online interactive game, you are in the minority. In the United States, games generate almost twice the revenue of movies. The biggest-selling video game, *Pokémon*, has grossed over $90 billion compared to the number one movie of all time, *Avatar*, at less than $3 billion.[20] Ryan explains, "Games have an incredible motivational pull. The better we understand the deeper psychology behind the palpable love people have for video games, the more we can harness that energy to enhance education, training, and social and leadership skills development."

But the experts at Immersyve warn against implementing gamification strategies without the insight of motivation science. Rigby points out, "Many companies rush too quickly to gamification, making the mistake of confusing the *tactic* of game mechanics as the *goal*. They turn internal websites for sales or human resources into games or contests that can often lead to ill-advised decisions to wrap glitzy badges and rewards around experiences. Those tactics not only don't *sustain* motivation or build value but can hurt the relationship with employees because it communicates that the value lies in the badges and points, rather than the substance of your business or the health of your employees."[21]

Rigby, Ryan, and Deci offer two critical pieces of advice if you are considering games and contests to "motivate" employees:

- *Don't begin with the goal to create a gamelike approach*—Begin with the intent to create a vehicle where people can be optimally motivated and sustain engagement. Rigby explains, "Thoughtful application of game design can facilitate an authentic satisfaction of people's psychological needs for choice, connection, and competence. Understanding the nature of human motivation is essential for communicating to employees that your organization and its offerings are where the value lies—not the badges and confetti sprinkled on top."
- *Think about motivation versus rewards*—The two concepts are very different and can be antagonistic. Research confirms that games based on reinforcing performance through rewards rather than recognizing and supporting optimal motivators do not result in enjoyment and immersion (which increase comprehension and competence), the likelihood a person will play next week (indicating sustained engagement, autonomy, and choice), or a preference to play more games by a particular developer (reflecting loyalty and connection).

According to Deci, who conducted the first studies of monetary rewards and intrinsic motivation, "Giving rewards to reinforce learning undermines short-term learning and long-term engagement in games—and goals in the workplace. However, people will find activities intrinsically *rewarding* and more deeply satisfying when their choice, connection, and competence are respected, encouraged, and supported by game elements—and their managers at work."

Despite the misuse of gamification in the workplace, wouldn't it be amazing if we could help people fulfill their psychological needs and experience optimal motivation through the games we play?

Rethink Rewards

As a fierce advocate of striving for optimal motivation instead of throwing tokens, badges, and rewards at people, I am armed and ready with scientific proof to answer the inevitable question I get during my presentations: Are rewards ever appropriate?

But thanks to compelling new research on the topic, I've softened my hard-line no. While I stand by the ineffectiveness of rewards to motivate and sustain behavior change, I now add three caveats to my answer.

Caveat #1: The Last Resort

Rewards may not be appropriate or the best choice for promoting the behavior you need from someone, but you might decide they are necessary.

In April 2022, the FBI announced a $10,000 reward seeking the public's help to find those responsible for pointing lasers at airplanes in flight near Seattle. The danger posed to pilots, passengers, and people on the ground was too great to ignore.[22] Selling out a friend for $10,000 is sad. But it's more pathetic not to do the right thing by stopping them or voluntarily turning them in without an incentive.

You might justify bribes when the stakes are high and the time line is short. But I still contend that rewards are a last resort only when people refuse to do the right thing for the common good.

Caveat #2: Reframe Incentives

Margie Blanchard is a cofounder of the Ken Blanchard Companies. Years ago, as president of the company, Margie became a fierce advocate of regular and formalized one-on-one meetings between managers and their employees to improve relationships and foster the company's flagship programs, SLII® and Self Leadership (in full disclosure, I'm the lead developer of Self Leadership with Ken Blanchard and Lawrence Hawkins).

Margie sheepishly explains what it took to make one-on-one meetings an integral part of the organization's culture: "We had to pay managers to do them. We paid each manager $200 per direct report for conducting biweekly one-on-one meetings. It's not something I am proud to admit, but I am proud that today these conversations are a centerpiece of our culture because people recognize their value."

Let me be quick to point out that Margie's approach worked not because she was paying people but because she framed her proposal in a way that enabled people to see it through an optimal motivational outlook. Her proposal: "We believe one-on-one meetings are so vital to building successful relationships, honoring our values, and being a role model to our clients that I am willing to pay you to do it for one year. After this year, I trust that the value of the practice will speak for itself." As a witness from the beginning, I can attest that this is precisely what happened.

If you need to sweeten the pot to get people to try what's good for them, be careful how you position the proposal. Be sure to do the following:

- Focus on the behavior you want to see.
- Demonstrate that you are empathetic about how individual concerns might be impacted.
- Perhaps most importantly, remind people that the reward is not a carrot to entice their compliance but a reflection of how strongly you believe in the benefit of the behavior.

Instead of offering money as an incentive, highlight the significance of what you're asking from people—to them and the organization.

Caveat #3: Make Rewards Meaningful

I just wrote about my chagrin with tokens and badges, but I thought I'd offer an example that worked.

I often shop at Jimbo's, a grocery store here in San Diego. Like most retailers, it faced the movement to reduce single-use plastic bags. Some states banned plastic bags, and some instituted a disincentive by charging extra for a bag.[23]

Jimbo's went a different route. It gives you one token per bag when you bring your own bags. Leaving the store, you drop your wooden coins into containers dedicated to local charities. Jimbo's then donates real money to charities based on the number of tokens collected. I can hardly wait to spend my coins. Sometimes all my tokens go to one charity. Oftentimes I can't decide, so I drop one coin into each container.

Jimbo's' simple token program works on multiple levels:

- It gets the behavior it hoped for because I rarely forget to bring my cloth shopping bags.
- It helps me fulfill my psychological need for choice (I choose not to use plastic or paper bags; I can donate to the charity I choose), connection (I feel good helping the environment and contributing to local charities), and competence (I leave the store feeling more effective at living my values—and grateful for following through on my good intentions).
- And finally, Jimbo's reinforces customer loyalty by creating a peak ending to my shopping experience. Research shows that powerful moments that stick have positive beginnings and endings.[24]

If you are as thoughtful as Jimbo's about offering rewards to encourage behavior change, I might reconsider my answer to the question, "Are rewards ever appropriate?"

Rethink Trust

The concepts of trust and motivation are interrelated— and understanding their integration is essential for getting the results you seek from your team while promoting their flourishing.

When you trust another person, you have positive expectations regarding their behavior and intentions. You are willing to be vulnerable to them and their promises.[25] Note the word *willing*. Trust is a volitional act: you choose to trust or not trust someone else. Since trust is a choice, your motivation to trust affects how you encourage choice, deepen connection, and build competence.

Motivation science inspires us to rethink trust in the workplace in three ways.

1. Motivation and Your Propensity to Trust

Trust is a two-way street. You trust people to do a job; people trust you to provide them with the resources they need to do the job. For example, let's say you don't trust one of your team members despite his track record of good performance. Because you somehow can't trust him entirely, you hesitate to grant him the authority or training he needs to make decisions on his own. Your lack of trust eventually erodes the person's sense of autonomy and choice, but it also negatively affects his connection to you and his self-perception of competence.

When you lack trust in the people you lead, you effectively erode their psychological needs and the likelihood for them to experience optimal motivation. And, of course, we know that people's productivity and sustained performance depends on the quality of their motivation.

One adage advises that to encourage others to trust you, you must take a leap of faith and extend your trust to them first. Indeed, research finds that when a leader scores low on the propensity to trust others, others are less likely to find that leader trustworthy.[26]

But your trusting others requires a skillful evaluation of their ability to accept what you trust them to do. Even more challenging, your propensity to trust may be hampered by your experience. Trust is a historical concept. For example, you might have been burned by delegating an important project to someone who failed to deliver. That awful experience eroded your sense of connection because you felt betrayed by the person's lack of effort. Or maybe your sense of competence was shattered, and now you question your ability to delegate effectively.

Ask yourself, What's your motivation to trust? How has your motivation to trust been shaped by past experiences? Your propensity to trust others might be trigger-sensitive because choice, connection, or competence were undermined in the past. If you've ever been challenged to start dating again after a bad breakup, you know what I mean! The question is, Are you willing to surrender to the possibility of facing similar pain again so you can move on and step into something more meaningful?

2. Motivation and Your Team Members' Propensity to Trust

Like you, the people you lead may carry the baggage of unfulfilled needs, so their propensity to trust is affected by their historical experiences.[27] If that's not enough to concern you, motivation research shows a correlation between employees' trust in their leaders and the degree to which their psychological needs are met at work.[28] Their ability to trust you as a leader is significantly affected by how well your workplace implements motivation science, making it more or less likely for them to experience optimal motivation.

The interrelationship between motivation and trust is profound: people's fulfillment of choice, connection, and competence—whether from the environment, you, or themselves—opens up their ability to trust others.

Leadership involves an exchange of influence between people. Your leadership capacity to encourage choice, deepen connection, and build competence is fundamental to trusting relationships where people feel safe, seen, and heard. But it's also essential for people to see you as trustworthy.

3. The Dark Side of Motivation and Trust

A work environment that cultivates choice, connection, and competence is one thing. But an environment that thwarts these needs is another. A perilous dark side exists where trust intersects with people's psychological needs. According to motivation science, employees' trust in their leader is *inversely* related to how much employees feel their psychological needs are being thwarted at work. Said differently, the more employees' choice, connection, and competence are thwarted, *the less* they will trust their leader.[29]

Where you find toxic workplaces, you find need-thwarting environments. In her book *Bad Leadership,* Barbara Kellerman reveals need-thwarting leader behaviors, including callous behavior (e.g., lack of kindness or attention to what others want), corruption (e.g., lying, stealing), insularity (e.g., favoring members of an in-group), or evil behaviors (e.g., causing pain to keep power over others).[30]

As millions of job seekers will attest as they attempt to escape, toxic workplaces are dysfunctional and lack psychological safety. Instead of people trusting each other, they clam up or keep their heads down to protect themselves. They start to look out for their own interests and stop taking personal risks for the team's sake. The quit-and-stay phenomenon won't disappear until toxic workplaces do. The truth also dies in darkness as people will never speak their truth to power.

The sad truth is when psychological needs are thwarted, people are no longer willing to be vulnerable to others—making trust impossible.

Psychological Sense to the Rescue

Leading with psychological sense involves balancing and honestly processing your inner experiences and environment. That means you can pinpoint positive emotional states. But it *also* means you can notice, acknowledge, and accept your challenging, less favorable emotional states. If you have the muscle to withstand your own tough emotions, you can be a pillar of strength for others who come to you as they process theirs. Your psychological sense will help you practice the three leadership capacities to support people's needs and self-regulate to avoid the abusive or destructive behaviors that thwart their needs.

Your motivational leadership affects trust going and coming. You lay the foundation for trust to grow between you and your team when you encourage choice, deepen connection, and build competence. In return, your optimally motivated team members deem you trustworthy because you helped them fulfill their psychological needs for choice, connection, and competence.

A Case in Point: Rethinking Employee Engagement

Alvar Piera is aspirational. As the commercial learning and development senior manager at Beckman Coulter Dx Europe, he has an unyielding belief that educating leaders at all levels in an organization is the key to unlocking the potential in every human being. But he isn't naive. He understands the pressure for executives to demand results, especially in publicly held companies. He appreciates the burden managers feel in executing strategies that achieve those results.

But after decades of management positions in international sales, training, and continuous improvement, Alvar also grasps how ineffective traditional methods of motivation are for generating and sustaining the high performance required to do what executives and managers are asking people to do.

Alvar explains, "Year after year, many managers witness the same theme: How do we do more with less? How do we sell more at better margins with fewer resources, follow lean management processes, and optimize everything? Managers are constantly being held accountable to hit more challenging targets. The managers are beyond stressed, and people are beyond exhausted—and we have data to prove it.

"Like many companies, we measure engagement. We have annual objectives and a process to manage objectives. Then we realize we have an engagement gap. That's when managers jump to motivation as a solution. But because they don't understand the connection between engagement and motivation, they resort to external motivation, incentives, and bonuses to engage people. They tend to believe their only recourse to improve engagement is manipulating or bribing people into it."

Alvar wants managers to rethink their approach to employee engagement. His rethinking began after reading my first book on motivation. Now he poses to others the question that reshaped his understanding of engagement and motivation: where does engagement come from?

As Alvar understands firsthand, organizations spend a ton to measure, analyze, and build plans around a phenomenon that researchers have only recently explored: how people become engaged.[31] "Companies are doing all this work to improve engagement without understanding its root cause. How can you fix an engagement problem if you don't understand how individuals become disengaged or engaged in the first place?" Alvar asks.

The cutting-edge research Alvar took to heart shows how individuals are constantly appraising the workplace by consciously and subconsciously asking, "Do I feel safe or threatened? Am I energized or enervated? Do I feel negative or positive?" This appraisal leaves them feeling positive well-being or negative ill-being. Whatever they conclude determines their intentions—those intentions become the most significant predictors of behavior.[32] A positive appraisal that results in a positive sense of well-being leads to positive intentions and behaviors that generate employee engagement. A negative appraisal leads to disengagement.[33]

Alvar's aha moment came with the realization that when people are optimally motivated, they tend to have a positive appraisal that leads to high engagement. When they experience suboptimal motivation, they are more likely to go down the path to disengagement. The research Alvar refers to is summarized in figure 5.1.[34]

In figure 5.1, the plus symbols reflect a significant positive correlation between optimal motivation and the five intentions that lead to employee work passion, the no signs indicate no significant correlation between suboptimal motivation and the five intentions, and the minus signs signify a significant negative correlation between the disinterested motivational outlook and the five intentions that lead to employee disengagement.

Alvar reinforces the message whenever he can and hopes managers take the message to heart: "Optimal motivation fuels employee work passion; suboptimal motivation fuels disengagement. I support Susan's assertion that motivating people doesn't work, but that managers play an essential role in people's appraisal process. By rethinking their approach to motivation, managers can encourage choice, deepen connection, and build competence so people are more likely to experience the day-to-day optimal motivation that leads to engagement and employee work passion."[35]

A reality that Alvar accepts is that, like most managers, he needs to work within his realm of control, to do what he can to set up an environment where people can be more optimally motivated. "I don't have the position or power to change everything in my organization. But what I can do is find champions, work with early adopters, and make small changes that might

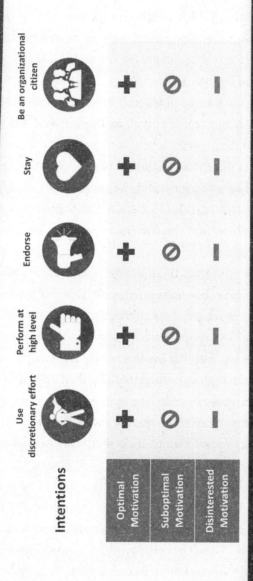

FIGURE 5.1 The Business Case for Optimal Motivation

have a positive ripple effect. I know we won't change the paradigm overnight, but I'm on a mission to teach managers the truth about motivation and how the quality of a person's motivation fuels either disengagement or employee work passion."

Alvar knows his mission includes working on his own motivation. Alvar lives according to one of my cherished life mottos: "I teach what I most need to learn." He laughs, recalling, "I had to begin with myself. When talking to a colleague about an initiative I disagreed with, I used to say, 'I'm not motivated.' Or, we would ask each other, 'Okay, between zero and ten, how motivated are you to work on this goal?' I had to rethink my own motivation. Now I ask myself, what's my motivational outlook? Is my motivation suboptimal or optimal? Do I need to create choice, connection, or competence?"

You cannot deny Alvar's passion for sharing what he learns with others. He notes: "For the sake of people's health and their own, managers need to rethink the way they lead. To that end, I want to teach them the leadership capacities to improve people's psychological sense so they can experience choice, connection, and competence and generate the optimal motivation to thrive and be effective under any circumstances."

Recapping "Rethinking Leadership Now That Everything Else Has Changed"

We have the greatest opportunity, perhaps in history, to transform the way we work—to create a workplace where producing results doesn't undermine people's health and well-being. People can be effective and flourish when equipped with psychological sense—the emotional and cognitive ability to fulfill psychological needs and experience optimal motivation, thriving, and sustained high performance.

The leadership imperative is applying the three leadership capacities to set goals, provide feedback, and deal with issues ranging from hybrid work to gamification. When leaders encourage choice, deepen connection, and build competence, the people they lead are more likely to develop the psychological sense that empowers them to thrive wherever they work and be resilient no matter what changes the future demands.

6

Leader, Heal Thyself

Years ago, I met with Dr. Edward Deci, recognized as the father of and leading researcher in the field of intrinsic motivation—and one of my heroes. My purpose was to get his reaction to the Spectrum of Motivation and our approach to motivation. I explained, "We imagine a whole new world at work where every individual accepts responsibility and takes the initiative for creating their own optimal motivation."

After studying the model and descriptions for mastering motivation, Deci paused. I was so relieved when he announced, "We are simpatico." Buoyed by his endorsement, I explained that we also wanted to teach managers leadership capacities to facilitate people's optimal motivation.

Pause, long pause. Finally, he said, "Okay. But with a caveat. Leaders must understand how to shift their own motivation before they can hope to guide others." He shook his head warily: "Can you imagine a manager who hates performance reviews conducting a review to help employees shift their motivation? It will not end well."

> "Leaders must understand how to shift their own motivation before they can hope to guide others."

I agreed, but immediately ran into a roadblock: teaching leaders about motivation was challenging because they believe their job is to motivate the people they lead—not themselves. Despite that widespread belief, I've been privileged to work with leaders who dare to look inward before working outward.

I hope you find the stories of these extraordinary leaders as inspiring as I have.

Amber Barnes on Vulnerability

Amber Barnes is the founder of StartHuman in Reno, Nevada, an organization dedicated to rehumanizing the workplace and beyond through an interdisciplinary approach to coaching, training, facilitation, and consulting.

Have you met someone who immediately rubs you the wrong way? That same phenomenon happens when you meet Amber Barnes—but in reverse. A few minutes into a conversation, you begin to notice a change, not in her but yourself. Without warning, you experience an intriguing combination of calm vitality. How does she do it?

Amber has worked diligently to become the human she wants to be. Unlike entrepreneurs and executives who rub you the wrong way by leading with ego and false promises, she rubs off on you positively with her authenticity and sense of gratitude—making you feel better about yourself.

I'm convinced that Amber's gift lies in the psychological sense she's developed through her unique perspective blending various bodies of work, including that of Dr. Brené Brown, with the motivation framework described in this book and *Master Your Motivation*.

Amber says, "You've defined motivation as the energy to act. So when I'm stuck—when I lack the energy to move forward on something or my thought process is so fragmented I can't think straight—it's a cue to stop and reflect: Which of my psychological needs is not being met: choice, connection, or competence?"[1]

Not long ago, Amber realized she was stuck and pinpointed the cause: she was missing connection with people who mattered to her. But then she went a step further. As she describes it, "I asked myself why my need for connection wasn't being fulfilled. I realized that I had walled myself off and stopped communicating my needs to people. I was suffering from vulnerability avoidance. That's where Brené's work came in.

"When I understood that the fear of feeling vulnerable was blocking me from experiencing connection, I was able to create a breakthrough. Being vulnerable is an emotion. After acknowledging an emotion, we can mindfully choose to feel it, and move through it."

Feeling vulnerable is a normal human emotion. Amber's motivation shifted when she realized that her fears and concerns didn't mean she was broken. They just meant she was real. Amber explains, "When I stopped hiding my struggles and authentically shared when my feelings were hurt, I surprisingly started experiencing more connection." Amber expresses an irony confirmed by motivation science: "The more connection I have with myself, the more connection I can create with others."

Using the skill of motivation, Amber recognized she had choices about how she wanted to show up. She could self-protect with armor (ways we foster disconnection and avoid vulnerability), or she could choose to be openhearted and share her truths.

Amber says, "When I make a choice to lean into vulnerability and see it as a strength rather than a weakness, I'm more likely to have authentic connections with people I care about. Then I realize 'Wow, this feels good.' I love that I'm able to be more autonomous—and I experience a wave of competence because I'm growing and making progress. I feel grateful for all the tools in my toolbox that are applicable and relevant for not only me in my own.life but my clients too."

Amber's psychological sense comes from embracing vulnerability and using it as a catalyst to create the choice, connection, and competence that leads to well-being, a sense of agency, and optimal motivation. Her skill at shifting her motivational outlook serves her well as she teaches conscious leadership to managers and executives.

"So many leaders think they can fake it till they make it. My message to those leaders: People can sniff that stuff out. You're not fooling anyone but yourself," Amber says.

Teaching leaders to acknowledge, embrace, and lean into vulnerability is core to Amber's approach to leadership development. She positions vulnerability as an emotion we need the capacity to feel and experience in order to get our psychological needs met. She believes that only by dealing with your own needs are you capable of helping people fulfill theirs.

I am struck by Amber's words of wisdom to leaders, shaped by personal experience: "When we struggle and work through our discomfort, we become much kinder and more compassionate with others. We hear the words that signal a person feels trapped without a choice. We understand the language that reflects someone's loneliness, longing, or disconnection. We read between the lines, sensing when they feel stuck, stagnant, incompetent, or inadequate.

"I'm a better coach, a better trainer, and a better consultant because I've done the hard work of self leadership. Great leaders don't say, 'Be like me.' They use their tools to help people create vitality and be their best selves. That's the magic of conscious leadership."

Dr. Beth Scalone on the Motivation Trifecta

Dr. Beth Scalone owns North County Water and Sports Therapy Center in San Diego, California. She is an orthopedic specialist, certified Pilates instructor, and international consultant on aquatic physical therapy.

As the sole proprietor of a small business, Beth has learned that practicing motivational leadership is three times a challenge.

Beth's first motivation challenge is working with patients and their problems, like me. I've been Beth's physical therapy patient through minor and major surgeries, including a knee replacement. Oh, the stories she could tell. But this is my book, and I get to tell stories about Beth.

Named the national Aquatic Therapy Professional of the year, Beth's competence in healing her clients has never been questioned. But Beth realized many of her clients suffered from not complying with her recommendations. She struggled getting people to do what was in their own best interest. She decided to try my framework to guide those difficult conversations with people.

As Beth explains, "I use Susan's mindful questions with patients when they have difficulty being compliant with their home program or being consistent with their therapy appointments." Through the questions, Beth's clients may discover they don't understand the purpose of the exercise (lack connection) or don't know if they are doing it correctly (lack competence). Beth has learned when it comes to the choice people make about their health, she can be honest without judgment and let them know the consequences of their choice.[2]

I have to laugh when I've given Beth an excuse for not doing my exercises between our sessions and catch her using my stuff on me. But it also thrills me because it works!

Beth's second motivation challenge is working with her staff. She admits a big difference between being a good therapist and being a good leader of other therapists. She's not kidding. When I interviewed Beth for my first book, she told me, "I've learned to be patient with my patients, but I am not prone to mollycoddling my employees. As a manager, my attitude is 'Like it, lump it, and get on with it.'"

Times have changed. Beth begins integrating motivation science in the hiring process: "I ask a potential clinical team member why they chose to enter the field of physical therapy and how they feel about that choice. This leads to a conversation about what they love—their values. And it can also lead to what they dislike and if they will be a good fit."

Beth has a clear set of values, a sense of purpose, and a strong work ethic, so by asking potential new hires mindful questions that reveal their motivation for physical therapy, it becomes evident whether the applicant will fit. When Beth hires therapists, they become part of the family from the start and feel a sense of connection.

But Beth also recognizes that her staff's daily optimal motivation is essential to their well-being and the energy they share with their patients. She often finds herself having motivational conversations with them about topics as varied as putting equipment back in place to how they're dealing with a difficult client.

Beth is a skilled teacher who provides ongoing training and education for her staff. But she also embraces their competence by empowering them to use their own style to work with their clients, meet the demands of insurance companies, and keep the clinic humming. She encourages her staff to give *her* feedback on how she can be a better boss. She and her office manager even agreed on a code word to use if Beth's actions undermined her choice, connection, or competence.

Beth admits, "At the end of the day, it's humbling to be an owner and realize that when you give people the freedom to do good work, they will. They make me look good!"

Beth's third challenge is herself. Beth admits that the pandemic years were hard: "I had to remind myself why I chose to run a private practice. With each hard decision, I reminded myself that I had a choice—I might not like all the options, but I had the choice. Recognizing I was in control of my choices returned power to my hands and helped me avoid becoming the victim. When I asked myself why I was making my choices, I got in touch with my connection to my patients and clients. When I align my choices to my values, a sense of purpose, and the contribution I'm making to my client's health, I find myself making the right choices."

Praising risks enticing people with external motivation, so I will refrain from praising Beth. Instead, I will practice what I teach by expressing gratitude. Beth's values for contributing to the welfare of others are utterly transparent. But she's often pulled toward suboptimal motivation by the demands of running a small business—from regulations, paperwork, and financial obligations to needing more space and granting greater employee benefits. I'm grateful to have Beth as a role model for consciously choosing to shift her motivation so she can continue to be of service and grow as a leader.

Beth deserves the bounty that accompanies a trifecta of experiencing optimal motivation with clients, staff, and herself.

Brock Weatherup on the Year That Changed Everything

Brock Weatherup is on the boards of PetShopBowl UK and TrustedHousesitters, an active angel and seed stage investor in over twenty-five consumer-focused start-ups, and an operating partner at MidOcean Partners. "It never occurred to me that one day I'd wake up sick and never get better," Brock posted as he publicly announced he had been living with an aggressive form of multiple sclerosis (MS) for the past year.

As the wildly successful founder of companies like Fathead and PetCoach, Brock is known for making savvy business choices. But during the year that changed everything, his choices reflected more: the leadership capacity that inspired his team and the psychological sense empowering his personal journey. His wisdom can enrich each of us—no crisis required.

Brock's leadership capacity begins with this philosophy: "I don't want anybody to be working for me. I want them to be working with me." Over the past year, Brock learned that working hard to build your team pays off—or as he says, "Is a 1000x ROI." Brock urges leaders not to skimp on that investment, reminding us that our team includes family, friends, and professional relationships.[3]

When it comes to encouraging choice, Brock understands that people need to feel like they have a voice. Leaders must convey, "I hear you, I value you, and I trust you to make that decision." He says, "Everybody wants to feel that they control their destiny. If your employees think about their job 24/7/365, great. But it can't be because you've asked them to but because they want to." Brock admits if people want to follow orders, then working with him might not be their best choice.

Physical pain and discomfort accompany his disease. But he'll tell you that he suffered significant emotional distress over the best way to deal with his team—who had worked with him for years on other ventures. The day he was diagnosed, his thoughts were "What do I do with my team? I knew I would be a terrible leader for a bit because I was fully distracted. But then, I thought, these people know me, and they're not going to be mad at me for stepping out."

Brock pulled the leadership team together in an act that deepened connection more than he could imagine. As he describes it, "I was 100 percent open with them. I told them, 'Hey, guys, this just happened to me. I don't know what it means. I'm confused as hell. I'm scared, I'm terrified. I will not be the leader you need me to be to take our company to the next level because I'm going to be wildly distracted. I don't know what that means for me and this company's future. And I'm sorry about that. But let me deal with me. You guys deal with the business. I need you to own it.'"

Brock did his best to stay as involved and active as his MS allowed. Months later, the leadership team engaged in a robust planning strategy. Brock's approach to planning was not to give the team a direction but to collaborate. It wasn't as easy as it sounds. Brock's personality type prefers to make decisions. But his psychological sense enabled him to rise above his need to control. He's convinced that the reason some leaders fail to create choice, connection, and competence is that the behavior required goes against their nature. Too many leaders aren't willing to expend the energy to change their instinctive behavior in service of their values.

Brock was celebrating his team's competence, reveling in the decisions they were making, and feeling proud of the quality human beings they were when his body finally failed him. He couldn't see. His hands wouldn't work. "That's when I realized I needed to let go of the team and the business—and I could. My team could handle it. Ironically, it was the deep connection with my team and their competence that gifted me with the choice to do the right thing for everyone."

Brock's psychological sense begins with being genuine. "It's an easy term to throw around but a tough thing to demonstrate," he admits. "People can't trust a leader who isn't genuine. But being genuine is also essential to your health and well-being."

He elaborates, "This will sound like an egotistical statement, but I think I'm pretty talented. I'm not bragging. For me, that's a genuine statement. You can't be genuine without self-awareness. That means acknowledging your strengths— and facing your weaknesses. When you are aware of your strengths and weaknesses, you can be intentional and forthright. Self-awareness and intention enable you to explore and celebrate your team's strengths and weaknesses."

Entering year two of his new life, Brock reflects, "I think what surprises me most is the realization that I'm a better man today than I was a year ago. I have colleagues I now consider friends. I've always appreciated my family, but my love has deepened to unexpected levels. I want to think that I was always sensitive to those less fortunate than I am, but my empathy has increased multifold. You do not know what someone else is dealing with—just because you don't 'see it' doesn't mean it isn't heavy and hard.

"Today, I am satisfied with the choices I've made but even more grateful for the choices I have. I'm more connected through a community of like-minded and values-based family and friends. And I'm more appreciative of the competence I've gained to deal with this degenerative disease with some measure of grace."

Brock's experience makes me wonder, What if we thought about the upcoming year as the year that changed everything? What might life be like if we recognized and appreciated our choice, connection, and competence each day? Could our positive vitality radiate, giving others the gift of hope and resilience? If Brock is any indication, the answer is an emphatic yes.

Karen Adams on Facing Fears

Karen Adams is a CEO with international and multi-industry experience and winner of Canada's 100 Most Powerful Women by Women's Executive Network in 2017 and CEO of the Year by *Wealth Professional* in 2019.

Alberta Pensions hired Karen Adams as its CEO because it needed an agent of change. But that didn't mean everyone was jumping on board for the ride. Karen explains, "A virtual unknown to the longtime employees of this venerable organization, I was hired to bring the company into the future. But everyone had their own opinions about what that future should be. My mission was to lead a staid manual processing paper-based organization through a technological transformation that would change how everybody did everything. Talk about motivation."[4]

Karen realized she couldn't motivate one person, a team, or an entire organization. But she knew she could drive a culture suboptimally motivated by the promise of power, more money, and status—or pressure people through fear and threats. Instead, she focused her leadership on developing a core group of people aligned with her proposed values and vision. This optimally motivated team provided Karen with the safe space she needed to form her strategy and execution plans.

After serious preparation, Karen and her team announced their first corporate summit to convey their plan to the company. Karen describes the scene: "We packed four hundred employees into our local Cineplex theater. We fit perfectly. Then, we put on a show. We dressed up as characters and did silly bits about our plans for the future and why they were so exciting. It was funny and self-deprecating."

But what Karen did next was inspired and inspiring. In her words, "I said to everyone, look, I'm asking you to do something pretty big. Changing the status quo and transforming the organization is a big deal. It's easy for me to say it, but you're the ones who have to do it. You are the ones who have to make the change.

"I know you may fear all these changes. I understand because I'm afraid of something too—like really, really afraid of. Needles. I hate needles. I've never given blood, even though I've always wanted to, because I've always been too scared. So, in your honor, I'm going to give blood."

Karen invited people to join her in donating blood at the Alberta blood bank. She admitted she was scared, but the blood banks were in need, and they could help.

Then, realizing people needed a chance to process what they'd heard, they watched a movie and ate popcorn together.

People did join Karen at the blood bank bus—people like her who were afraid and had never done it before. And they all felt like heroes.

Karen took motivation science seriously. She encouraged choice through her noncontrolling language, inviting people to change. She built competence through an organized and thoughtful plan of action that provided the information people needed to understand how the changes would affect their roles and everyday work. And she deepened connection in three ways. Karen and her team formulated a strategy based on a solid sense of purpose, meaningful values, and contribution to the greater good (for employees and the community they serve). The fun rollout of the change initiative deepened connection as people celebrated, laughed together, and shared a movie and popcorn. But the most profound connection came through her vulnerability when Karen modeled overcoming the fear of change.

Promoting optimal motivation didn't end with Alberta Pensions. Once that transformation was complete, Karen moved on to another organization needing change. That's what she does—she wields her executive power to get results. But what makes her—and the organizations she serves—successful is the way she taps her power through her leadership capacity to encourage choice, deepen connection, and build competence every step of the way.

Mike Easley on Drilling Deep

Mike Easley is a former CEO, consultant, author, executive coach, gigging musician, and soon-to-be therapist. Mike is a recovering engineer with an MBA in business, and a master's degree in clinical mental health counseling.

Talk about the Wild West. Powder River Energy Corporation (PRECorp), headquartered in Sundance, Wyoming, is a cooperative that brings energy to rural areas too remote for a public utility company to bother with. That isolation was a catalyst for CEO Mike Easley and his leadership team to institute a strategic execution model that yielded 20 percent value added to his cooperative's members. Ask Mike how he generated such success in this rugged world of energy, power, and cowboys who happen to be linemen. You learn that the perceived isolation became a catalyst for personal growth and business success.

Mike reached a turning point in his career in 2011, when he decided to leave PRECorp and embark on a job search. When his dream job fell through, he sank into a funk. During this time, he was asked to provide the music for a religious service at a local nursing home, something he'd done in the past. That particular evening, the minister didn't make it. Mike conducted the service, led prayers, and played his guitar. It was a life-changing moment. Mike says he experienced a meaningful connection with each individual in the service and his music. He felt a deep sense of joy from contributing to the welfare of others.

That night in the nursing home, Mike recognized how hungry he had been for a sense of connection. He made visiting the nursing home a weekly ritual and began playing regularly at nursing homes and assisted living facilities. He started to challenge his introverted nature and found himself conversing more freely. It dawned on him that he was one Mike, not a group of compartmentalized Mikes—one guy at home, another at work, and another when playing music to senior citizens. He was eager to experience connection, especially to himself. He wanted the joy he felt at the nursing home in other parts of his life. As it turned out, allowing himself to be more vulnerable improved everything—his music, writing, singing, compassion, and empathy for others.

Mike was an early adopter of the ideas in this book. His entire leadership team attended beta tests of the original workshop, so he recognized what was happening. He realized that his job searching had been a quest for connection. Being CEO of PRECorp fulfilled two psychological needs: With his executive power, he had choice. With all his years of experience, he had competence. Mike didn't need a new job; he needed a sense of connection at PRECorp.

Mike returned his energy to the energy organization he had been so ready to leave. He implemented a visioning process. He involved PRECorp employees in a video discussing Powder River Energy's role in their lives and the community. He worked with the board to change his role, passing most of his operational duties to a new COO so he could focus on building a new culture and developing the PRECorp leadership team. Mike wanted others to experience connection at work.

With their standout results, Mike's team trained other energy co-ops throughout the United States on PRECorp's new strategic execution system—they were dedicated to strengthening the entire industry. Mike continues to reflect on his turnaround: "I never want to settle. Yet I want to be at peace and continue to grow. I think leaders need to develop the skills they hope their employees and teammates will have. If you want to be a leader worth following, you need to be able to lead yourself first. I don't want to look over my shoulder at the end of my career and see any carnage left behind."[5]

In early 2019, Mike reminded his board that his employment contract would end in late 2020 and asked if they would like to extend the agreement now rather than wait. They declined, kicking that ball down the road. With his future in question, Mike faced an existential crisis threatening his choice, connection, and competence. He floundered until a trusted friend and mentor suggested he take charge of his life and be in a position by late 2020 to make his own choices about his future.

Mike discovered that being a CEO was what he did, not who he was. By the time the contract term expired, Mike had written two books, one on leadership and another on how to heal yourself after a dysfunctional relationship. He was also enrolled in a master of science in clinical mental health counseling program. Mike did agree to extend his PRECorp contract, but only long enough to effect a seamless transition to new leaders committed to the leadership development process he had implemented.

After twenty years as a CEO, Mike is now actively engaged in climbing his "second mountain," pursuing a career helping others as a professional executive and life coach. He holds that creating an optimally motivating workplace and practicing the skill of motivation for himself were critical to his leadership success. Mike shares, "By being aware of our internal state, we can create the choice, connection, and competence we need to keep ourselves optimally motivated. Only then will we be the gentler, kinder, and nicer version of ourselves—and a leader worth following."

Recapping "Leader, Heal Thyself"

The leaders in this chapter are exceptional, but I'm thrilled that leaders willing to challenge traditional leadership are becoming less rare. More and more leaders appreciate the role they play in people's motivation and work passion. They see the value in nurturing a flourishing and effective workplace by applying their leadership capacity to encourage choice, deepen connection, and build competence. But as Deci advised years ago—and as the leaders portrayed in this chapter demonstrate—before you can facilitate anyone else's psychological sense and optimal motivation, you need to tend to your own.

7

Are Your Beliefs Eroding People's Optimal Motivation?

Motivation is one of the most vital aspects of leadership and also one of the most confused and misunderstood. This confusion and misunderstanding makes leaders blind to what does and doesn't work. They engage in counterproductive behaviors, believing they are doing the right thing. Leaders are so immersed in five motivation-eroding beliefs that they find it difficult to hear, see, or do something different.

Research over the past sixty years continues to prove the point. Individuals' rankings of workplace motivators are compared to their managers' rankings of what they think motivates them. The results reflect how most individuals feel: managers do not know what motivates their people. Managers tend to attribute external motivation to employees (actions not within the employees' control)—such as good wages, promotions, and job security. On the other hand, employees prefer more internal motivation (actions within the employees' control)—such as interesting work, growth, and learning.[1]

Why the big disconnect? One reason is that leaders do not have access to someone else's internal state of motivation, only their own. That could explain why managers tend to attribute internal motivations to themselves while at the same time judging others to be externally motivated. However, when it comes to their employees, leaders depend on their observations of external behaviors and conditions to evaluate people's motivation. Unfortunately, many leaders are not perceptive observers or wise interpreters of what they see, making it nearly impossible to understand someone's internal state of motivation by observing their external behavior.

To make understanding people's motivation even more confounding, different people can interpret the same conditions differently. For example, in a team meeting where all the members are asked to share personal information, you can find all six motivational outlooks being played out. The leader needs to find ways of shaping the request and the environment so that people are more likely to experience an optimal rather than suboptimal motivational outlook.

Research suggests another reason for the disconnect in the ranking of motivators between employees and their managers: employees don't understand the true nature of their own motivation. For example, an employee who feels she is trapped in her job, being taken advantage of, or overwhelmed by what is being asked of her may ask for more money. Under her breath, she is saying, "They don't pay me enough to put up with this." She doesn't understand that there will never be enough money to compensate for the void created when her psychological needs for choice, connection, and competence are not satisfied. People can't ask for what they don't know they need.

When leaders and their employees blame their workplace dissatisfaction on money, it creates three erroneous assumptions and detrimental actions:

- Even though people need and want money, believing it will make them happy distracts them from what genuinely brings them joy.
- Leaders typically don't have direct control over pay raises and rewards, so it lets them off the motivational hook. They throw their arms up in a leadership mea culpa and declare there's nothing they can do. Leaders may also use their lack of control over salaries and benefits as an excuse to avoid dealing with people's emotionally charged discontent.
- When people ask for more money or perks to compensate for their discontent, they perpetuate outdated beliefs about the role that money and rewards play in motivation.

The primary purpose of this chapter is to explore how your unexplored leadership beliefs could be influencing, and maybe even sabotaging, your approach to motivation.

Exploring Your Leadership Beliefs

Leaders are seldom asked to examine their beliefs. In the introduction to this book, I posed unfinished belief statements and asked you to consider how you would fill in the blanks. Here they are again:

- It's not personal; it's just _____.
- The purpose of business is to _____.
- Leaders are in a position of _____.
- The only thing that really matters is _____.
- If you cannot measure it, it _____.

Over the past decade, I have asked thousands of leaders representing dozens of languages to finish the sentences. No matter where the audience is from, they can yell out the completed phrase in unison. These beliefs are particularly sticky, so entrenched in organizational consciousness that we accept them without question. This poses a potential problem. Unexplored beliefs become the foundation for programmed values. Then these programmed values become the basis for rules, processes, procedures, actions, and, more seriously, your leadership behaviors.

Your mission, should you accept it, is to challenge these workplace beliefs, examine how they tend to undermine your people's optimal motivation, then consider alternative beliefs and best practices. I encourage you to shine a light on potentially unexamined values in the spirit of developing more meaningful motivational leadership values.

Challenge the First Eroding Belief: It's Not Personal; It's Just Business

Employees probably spend more waking hours interacting with their coworkers than family members. Yet managers believe their actions are not personal and just business. Every day you deliver information, feedback, or news to those you lead that affects their work, livelihood, opportunities, status, income, mood, health, or well-being. How is this not personal?

Whatever your beliefs, one thing is true: what you say as a leader *feels* personal to the people you lead. Therein lies the issue: feelings. Earlier in this book, we explored this word in organizations. Do you believe that expressing feelings does not belong in the workplace? If so, challenge yourself by asking, How did this belief become so commonly held? Where did *my* belief come from?

One possibility for why feelings are discouraged in the workplace is that managers don't feel competent to deal with them effectively. True, some employees do not self-regulate well and may let their emotions get the best of them from time to time. But the fear of unruly emotions is disproportionate to the occurrence and severity of emotional outbreaks.

What if you changed the belief that it's not personal, just business, to a belief more likely to promote optimal motivation? *If it's business, it's personal.*

Try embracing the idea that all emotions are acceptable, but not all behavior is acceptable. Notice, acknowledge, and deal with a person's emotions. Help others to self-regulate by practicing self-regulation for yourself. Listen to your heart and acknowledge the crucial role feelings play in your work and life. As your beliefs change, watch how your leadership capacity improves.

Challenge the Second Eroding Belief: The Purpose of Business Is to Make Money

When you believe that making money is the purpose of business, you are likely to focus on dashboard metrics instead of the people responsible for providing quality service to your customers and clients. You are apt to overemphasize results and pressure people to get those results. You may be tempted to employ questionable ethical practices. When given a choice, you might choose quantity over quality, short-term results over long-term outcomes, and profits over people.

How would your decisions and actions differ if you let go of believing that the purpose of business is to make money? Consider this optimal motivation belief: the purpose of business is to serve.

Think how this reframed belief might alter your organization's dashboard metrics—or at least the content and quality of the goals. Consider how your leadership would change if you reframed goals from focusing only on external customer service to including internal service, from focusing on results to improving the quality of effort to achieve those results, or from focusing on outcomes to emphasizing the growth and learning to produce the outcomes.

Hard-nosed businesspeople will push back on these ideas with a traditional argument: "You can serve all you want, but this soft stuff doesn't make you money, and if you don't make a profit, you will go out of business. Then you won't be serving anyone."

Yes, a business must make a profit to sustain itself. But to conclude that profit is the purpose of business is an illogical leap. You need air to live, plus water and food. But your life's purpose is not to just breathe, drink, and eat. Your purpose is richer and more profound than basic survival. The nobler your purpose and more meaningful your values, the more they influence *how* you live—and lead.

The nature of human motivation is not about making money. The nature of human motivation is in making meaning.

Making a profit or serving the people who serve your customers should never be an either-or decision. It is always both. But service comes before profit. To paraphrase what I have often heard Ken Blanchard proclaim, "Profit is the applause you get from creating an optimally motivating environment for your people so they want to take care of your customers."[2]

Definitive evidence shows that organizational vitality (measured by return on investment, earnings by share, access to venture capital, stock price, debt load, and other financial indicators) depends on employee work passion and customer devotion. It does not work the other way around—organizational vitality is *not* what determines customer devotion or employee work passion.[3]

Your organization prospers when you focus on fulfilling employees' psychological needs so they can serve customers' needs. An old sports analogy works equally well in business: focusing on profit is like playing the game with your eye on the scoreboard instead of the ball.

Challenge the belief that the purpose of business is to make money, and consider an optimal motivation belief: the purpose of business is to serve—both your people and your customers. Profit is a by-product of doing both of these well.

Watch how your people respond to your changed belief. When you believe that the purpose of business is to serve, you lead differently. Your decisions and actions are more likely to cultivate a workplace that supports people's optimal motivation. Then notice the results and accept the well-earned applause in the form of organizational vitality. Keep that in mind as you avoid practices that undermine people's psychological needs and encourage choice, deepen connection, and build competence instead.

Challenge the Third Eroding Belief: Leaders Are in a Position of Power

Imagine you work for a large organization. You catch the elevator to another floor and notice someone is already in it—the company's CEO. You have never met him, but you recognize him from company-wide meetings. Your heart might race a bit. You might think twice before you speak. You might feel excited at the opportunity to make his acquaintance, or you might feel worried about making a bad impression. Suffice it to say, if he was someone of lesser stature or if you hadn't recognized him as the CEO, the dynamic would be different.

"Managers need to be incredibly mindful and clear about the types of power they have and use. Most leaders will be surprised by the potentially negative emotional impact of having and using their power, in almost all its forms." These are the words of Dr. Drea Zigarmi, who found himself surprised by the strength of his research on how a leader's power affects people's motivational outlooks.[4] Even when you don't have intentions to use your power, just having it creates a dynamic that requires your awareness and sensitivity.

How Your Power Affects People's Motivation

Zigarmi, along with Dr. Taylor Peyton and myself, studied the use of power by leaders in the workplace.[5] You might find it helpful to consider the most commonly used types of power described below and the potential effect each one has on your people's emotional well-being, intentions, and motivational outlooks. What you discover might surprise you.

- *Reward power* is your power to promise monetary or nonmonetary compensation. There are two types of reward power.
- *Impersonal reward power* is the power to grant special benefits, promotions, or favorable considerations.
- *Personal reward power* is when your employees' feelings depend on being accepted, valued, and liked by you.

  Employees report that when they perceive any of the above three forms of reward power at work, they experience a suboptimal motivational outlook.

- *Coercive power* is your power to use threats and punishment if people fail to conform to desired outcomes. Understandably, coercive power usually results in a negative relationship between leader and follower—and a suboptimal motivational outlook. Leaders often see coercive power as the easiest, most expedient, and most justifiable form of power. Truly the junk food of power, coercive power creates a workplace where people must exercise high-quality self-regulation to avoid a suboptimal motivational outlook.

- *Referent power* is based on how your employees identify with you. Ironically, you may enjoy certain work relationships because your employees' self-identity is enhanced through interaction with you, their actions are based on their desire to be similar to and associated with you, or they think so highly of you that they are afraid to disagree with you. It might surprise you that when employees report that their managers have referent power, they often also report experiencing a suboptimal motivational outlook. Their dependence on you for their internal state of well-being tends to undermine their choice, connection, and competence.

- *Legitimate power* is bestowed through a position or title that gives a leader the justifiable right to request compliance from another individual. Having legitimate power is a blessing and a curse. You can do more good with it, but, as Spider-Man will tell you, "With great power comes great responsibility." You must be sensitive to how others perceive and integrate your legitimate power, lest, despite your good intentions, people interpret your power as diminishing their experience of choice, connection, and competence. Often referred to as *position power*, legitimate power manifests in various forms.

- *Reciprocity* stems from your employees feeling obligated to comply with your requests because you have done something positive for them.

- *Equity power*, thought of as quid pro quo, is when employees sense that you expect compensation for the work or effort you have put into the relationship.

- *Dependence power* is when your employees feel obliged to assist you because you're in need—not from a sense of connection but an imposed sense of social responsibility.
- *Expert power* comes through your depth and breadth of knowledge. Expert power relies on the perceptions your employees hold regarding your superior knowledge.
- *Information power* relies on your employees' perception of how you present persuasive material or logic.

  Even the last two types of power can result in employees reporting a suboptimal motivational outlook when they feel manipulated, threatened, or overwhelmed by your expertise or use of information (knowledge or power).

The bottom line is that using power tends to undermine people's psychological needs. It's not just your use of the power but also people's perception that you *have it* and *could use it*. Your power demands that people exert more energy to self-regulate and experience choice, connection, and competence. As Zigarmi puts it, "Power is very precious stuff. It entices the leader into flights of self-delusion and separateness from those they lead."[6]

If you are the CEO riding the elevator, you are not wielding power, but your title and assumed power changes the dynamic between you and the people you lead. What can a leader do then?

When Ken Blanchard was elected class president in the seventh grade, his father congratulated him. Then, he told him, "Now that you have power, don't ever use it. Great leaders are great because people trust and respect them, not because they have power." Theodore Blanchard was an admiral in the navy who told Ken that anyone who thinks that military-style leadership is my-way-or-the-highway leadership has never gone to battle. According to Admiral Blanchard, "If leaders acted like that, your men would shoot you before the enemy could."[7]

Using your power to motivate people won't work if you want them to experience optimal motivation. Shifting to an optimal outlook is something people can do only for themselves. But the workplace you create has an enormous influence on how successfully people will self-regulate, satisfy their psychological needs, and experience optimal motivation.

We need to change the belief that leaders are in a position of power. Consider this optimal motivation belief: leaders are in a position to empower others. You have the opportunity to empower people by encouraging choice, deepening connection, and building competence.

> **Consider this optimal motivation belief: leaders are in a position to empower others.**

When you avoid undermining practices and put your leadership capacity into practice, you focus your power on cultivating a workplace where your people, your organization, and you are reaping the rewards of optimal motivation.

Challenge the Fourth Eroding Belief: The Only Thing That Really Matters Is Results

At a recent speaking engagement, I asked, "How would you finish this statement: The only thing that really matters in business is *blank*?" The answer was so obvious that over three hundred people spontaneously filled in the blank by yelling in unison, "Results!"

I then asked them to consider the effect this tyranny of results has on the workplace. It was not easy. Leaders tend to tune out if you mess with results. Executives cannot imagine what matters at the end of the day besides results measured by dashboard metrics. I'm asking you what I asked of them—to consider alternatives to the traditional focus on results.

Redefine and Reframe Results

People want to achieve organizational metrics and assigned goals (when they are fair and agreed upon) but often interpret them as external or imposed. You can help people shift to an aligned motivational outlook by clarifying the underlying values behind your dashboard metrics. People may even shift to an integrated motivational outlook when metrics are authentically positioned as a means to fulfilling a noble purpose.

When Express Employment Professionals announced sales goals at a recent conference of franchise owners, the leaders reminded the attendees that the purpose of their business was to put a million people to work. The energy generated was electric! When Berrett-Koehler, my publisher, puts out its catalog of offerings to buyers, the cover's primary message is "A community dedicated to creating a world that works for all." My experience has been that every goal, metric, and decision pursued at Berrett-Koehler has that purpose at heart.

Framing results differently and trusting that individuals will still achieve necessary metrics will help people shift their motivational outlook.

Do Not Imply That Ends Justify the Means

If you believe results are what really matter without considering *why* those results are meaningful and *how* people go about
achieving them, you are, in essence, saying the ends justify
the means. What a sorry picture this paints. We do not need
the science of motivation to prove that means matter. In the
news, we witness scandals and horror stories of people, organizations, industries, and countries who prize ends over means
every day.

A graphic illustration is captured in the Academy Award–
nominated 2005 documentary *Enron: The Smartest Guys in the
Room*. You could read the book upon which it is based. But
you wouldn't hear the unnerving taped conversations between
giddy energy brokers celebrating as fires ravage California and
people are losing everything they own—and their lives. The
brokers knew the fires would spark higher energy demands
and prices, ensuring the results for which they were being held
accountable.

Enron is considered one of the ugliest business scandals in
American history. But it offers a more disturbing example of
what happens when people prize results more than the means
to achieve them. You ache for those who suffered at the hands of
the energy brokers but also for the brokers themselves, who were
addicted to motivational junk food so unhealthy it poisoned
their morals. The brokers were responsible for their actions,
which is why I advocate for individuals to master their motivation. However, the leaders were also responsible for creating a
culture based on beliefs that eroded choice, thwarted connection, undermined competence, and led to inhumane behavior.

A focus on results may yield short-term gains. However, those gains are at risk and compromised when people feel pressure, disconnected from meaningful goals, and used without an appreciation for their competence. The evidence is clear: people *can* achieve the results you seek, even if their psychological needs are thwarted. But their negative energy and lack of well-being make it rare for them to sustain or repeat those results—let alone exceed them.

Reframe the belief that the only thing that matters is results. Consider this optimal motivation belief: in the end, what really matters is not just the results people achieve but why and how they achieve them.

> **Consider this optimal motivation belief: in the end, what really matters is not just the results people achieve but why and how they achieve them.**

Observe the shift in people's energy—and your own—when you focus on what really matters in the workplace. Focus on meaningful results that fulfill people's psychological needs for optimal motivation. Then trust that the numbers will add up.

Challenge the Fifth Eroding Belief: If You Cannot Measure It, It Doesn't Matter

Setting measurable goals and outcomes is essential. Having a defined finish line in front of you can be positively compelling.

In chapter 5, I wrote about ensuring higher results through SMART goals where the *M* is changed to *motivating*. However, we also need to move beyond SMART goal setting and embrace aspects of work that are not easily measured.

The Nature of Things That Cannot Be Measured

Some parents have SMART goals for their child's education and development of skills. But how would you answer this question: What do you most hope for your child? Most parents tell me they hope their children experience meaningful relationships, enjoy a profound connection to the world, contribute to society, give and receive love, fulfill a noble purpose, are passionate about their work, discover what makes them happy, feel safe and secure, perceive they have choices, and can navigate and master the world around them.

The dreams parents most hope for their children cannot be easily measured. The same phenomenon happens when I ask leaders what they most wish for their people at work. They may use different terms, but they want a positive sense of well-being for their people. At the heart of what leaders hope for their people is fulfilling their psychological needs for choice, connection, and competence. Despite the deep knowledge of what they want for people, leaders still focus on what they can easily measure.

As in life, the most rewarding aspects of work are those most difficult to measure.

If you believe the statement "If you cannot measure it, it does not matter," ask yourself why. Is dealing with the emotional nature of things not easily measured outside your comfort zone? Do you believe your job is to control circumstances, and it's too overwhelming to manage something that's not easily measured?

Some Things Are Best Left Unmeasured

One of life's great joys is eating in Italy. Ask anyone who has traveled there—food tastes better in Italy. I had the profound experience of attending a weeklong cooking course in Tuscany. I say "profound" because it changed the quality of my life—not just my cooking but also my perspective on day-to-day living. The chef refused to provide exact measurements for anything he made. "How can I tell you how much water to put in the pasta dough? It depends on the quality of your flour and the kind of day—the temperature, the humidity. You must add some water and oil until it feels right." He was hesitant to commit to a menu or plan for the week. If the zucchini flowers were blossoming, we would have fried squash blossoms; if not, ripe tomatoes would become the centerpiece of a caprese salad.

The chef was teaching us mindfulness—to be present in the moment, notice the world around us, and be aware of our many options and choices. The food becomes a possibility for something more meaningful than nutrition. And people can taste the difference.

Of course, we must measure many aspects in life and at work. Pastries are a science, where measuring makes the difference between a fluffy cupcake and a hockey puck. But a growth step for leaders is to become more mindful of promoting dreams, ideals, and experiences that cannot be easily measured. That includes becoming more comfortable with feelings. If leaders rule out people's emotional nature at work—including their own—because they are not mindful or skilled enough to cope, we all lose what it means to be fully human. That is too high a price to pay for being comfortable.

Reframe the belief that if you cannot measure it, it is not important. Put this optimal motivation belief into practice: if you cannot measure it, it's probably really, really important.

> Put this optimal motivation belief into practice: if you cannot measure it, it's probably really, really important.

Observe the shift in energy when you apply your leadership capacity to focus on what cannot be easily measured—such as love, joy, and gratitude. Your people will eat it up.

Recapping "Are Your Beliefs Eroding People's Optimal Motivation?"

You cannot master the leadership capacity to fulfill people's psychological needs and improve their psychological sense with beliefs that erode choice, thwart connection, and undermine competence. Embrace beliefs that promote optimal motivation:

- If it's business, it's personal.
- The purpose of business is to serve.

- Leaders are in a position to empower others.
- In the end, what really matters is not just the results people achieve but why and how they achieve them.
- If you cannot measure it, it's probably really, really important.

Remember, not all beliefs are values, but all values are beliefs. Your values shape your leadership point of view, inform your decisions, guide your actions, and ultimately influence whether the people you lead experience suboptimal or optimal motivation.

> Remember, not all beliefs are values, but all values are beliefs. Your values shape your leadership point of view, inform your decisions, guide your actions, and ultimately determine whether the people you lead experience suboptimal or optimal motivation.

The Promise of Optimal Motivation

Being a leader is a privileged position. What you say, how you say it, and why you say it has meaning to your organization, the people you lead, and your personal experience.

The Promise of Optimal Motivation for Your Organization

Most leaders are stuck with systems that promote driving over thriving. Organizational systems are built on the faulty assumption that people need to be reinforced, rewarded, or driven to accomplish goals. They underestimate people's basic need to grow, excel, and contribute.

Even with the new science of motivation, many organizations will continue to perpetuate the Pecking Pigeon Paradigm—banking on motivating people through external means that appear expedient, easy, and controllable. The question is, At what cost? Escalating salaries, bonuses, and rewards are obvious costs. But when an organization focuses on rewarding the top 10 percent, what does it do to the motivation of the other 90 percent? What about the hidden costs of detrimental mental and physical health, absenteeism, and increased insurance rates, to name a few, wrought by traditional motivation's focus on motivational junk food? What about the opportunity losses in dedication, loyalty, creativity, and innovation?[1]

The time has come to consider the potential *opportunity gains* in teaching leaders and individuals the skill of motivation. What might happen if organizations expanded their traditional focus on results, performance, and productivity to focus on helping people fulfill their needs for choice, connection, and competence? What if leaders learned to avoid undermining practices and adopt the leadership capacity to encourage choice, deepen connection, and build competence? What if values were developed based on optimal motivation beliefs rather than outdated traditional beliefs?

> The time has come to consider
> the potential *opportunity gains* in
> teaching leaders and individuals
> the skill of motivation.

Answers to these questions could lead to a workplace where autonomous people hold *themselves* accountable, where meaningful relationships translate into organizational citizenship behaviors, and where competence leads to a learning organization rich with innovation, quality products and services, and streamlined processes.

When the ideas in this book move from theory into practice, a workplace full of passionate people with a positive sense of well-being is an opportunity and a promise.

The Promise of Optimal Motivation for the People You Lead

I ask executive audiences this question: "What do you want *from* your people?"

I get immediate and reasonable responses, such as "I want their focus, attention, effort, dedication, and loyalty" or "I want them to meet expectations, make their numbers, achieve their goals, do what I ask, and get results."

Then I ask a follow-up question: "What do you want *for* your people?"

It's funny how removing one letter from the question generates blank and dumbfounded stares. You see skepticism or even cynicism as they sense you are about to discuss some touchy-feely topic. With some prodding, the executives come up with what they want for their people: happiness, safety, security, health, fun, a sense of accomplishment, resilience, and peace.

I find these answers fascinating. The responses are similar to the characteristics of positive well-being. Yet leaders tend to focus on what they want *from* people, which undercuts well-being. They have it backward.

When you focus on what you want *for* people, you are more likely to get the results you want *from* people.

> When you focus on what you want *for*
> people, you are more likely to get the
> results you want *from* people.

The following personal experience reinforces the difference you can make when you encourage choice, deepen connection, and build competence.

Alexa was about to play either the final game of her high
school volleyball season or go on to the state championship. They
were playing their crosstown rival for the privilege of representing their division in the playoffs. Anyone involved in high school
sports knows it can get tense and exciting—and parents can be
more animated than the student athletes. Alexa's dad, Drea, and
I were shouting and jumping up with every point. In the best-of-
three series, the two teams were tied going into the third game. It
was do or die. This was side-out volleyball, meaning that the only
way a team could score was during a serve. The server would
continue serving until she lost the point. Alexa's team was
down, and it didn't look good. Then Alexa stepped up to serve.
It felt as if I was holding my breath during her entire service.

She won the first point. Then the second. Alexa's team
moved ahead, and they went on to win the game. Drea and I
were beside ourselves! I rushed down the bleachers to celebrate—I flew! Somehow, my husband beat me to Alexa, and
he was doing his Italian dad thing: kissing her on her forehead
and hugging her.

I was impatiently awaiting my turn. Finally, Drea stepped
back—I thought this was my chance. But with his hands on

Alexa's shoulders, he looked her directly in the eyes and asked, "Alexa, when you got up to serve, your team was losing nine to twelve. By the time you finished your serve, your team was ahead thirteen to twelve and went on to win the game. How did you feel about your serve tonight?"

I rolled my eyes and thought, "Stop talking; let me in there to celebrate!" Then I noticed something I had never witnessed before. Alexa's eyes began to glow. She said, "Dad! You know how I got frustrated with my serve and wanted to quit volleyball? But tonight, when I hit that overhead slam, I saw movement on the ball, and I knew there was no way they could return it. I got into the flow, and it was amazing! I am so happy for my team!"

At that moment, I realized the power of activating optimal motivation with others. In his wisdom, Drea first practiced the skill of motivation for himself. Through his high-quality self-regulation, he made the moment about Alexa and her experience, not his experience. What if I had gotten to Alexa first? I enjoy being excited and celebrating. Our conversation would have been about me: my excitement, pleasure, and interpretation of what just happened. I needed to reflect and ask myself, "Why are you excited? Whose experience are you celebrating?"

Had I gotten to Alexa before Drea, I could have undermined her psychological needs to satisfy my own. Drea self-regulated and acted on his love for his daughter. At that moment, he gave her a priceless gift.

Asking Alexa how she felt gave her the gift of *choice*—she had the opportunity to reflect on her interpretation of what happened and choose how she would remember it.

Drea gave her the gift of *connection*—he cared more about Alexa than his own need to express his excitement. He also allowed her to relate her outstanding performance to the team experience. She realized her joy wasn't about winning but her contribution to the team's success.

Drea also gave Alexa the gift of *competence*—for the first time in her teen years, I believe Alexa made the connection between hard work and results, effort, and outcome. She felt masterful at that moment. She will be able to recall and relish that sense of competence for the rest of her life.

Her father created a pocket of tranquility in an atmosphere where it would be easy to think the experience was only about winning. Alexa reflected and rejoiced in a deeper, more profound way. Don't get me wrong—she felt jubilation, but the reasons for feeling it shifted. An interaction between a father and daughter reinforced the power of optimal motivation, but the lesson learned is relevant for any workplace.

The Essence of the Promise of Optimal Motivation

A great irony of leadership is that motivating your people doesn't work because they are already motivated. People are always motivated. What works is embracing your leadership capacity to encourage choice, deepen connection, and build competence. By letting go of traditional motivation schemes, your leadership helps people develop and improve their psychological sense so they are more likely to experience optimal motivation. Your opportunity lies in facilitating people's shift to an optimal motivational outlook so they thrive and excel.

You also have a chance to master your own motivation. As an optimally motivated leader, you are more than a role model. Your vitality creates a positive ripple effect that fuels the optimal motivation that leads to employee work passion.

To appreciate the essence of optimal motivation, imagine people who choose to come to work because they experience a sense of positive well-being, feel that they are contributing to something greater than themselves, and are continually learning and growing. People can flourish as they succeed. This is the promise of optimal motivation.

Afterword

by Ken Blanchard

I have no doubt that the ideas you have just read will make
a difference in the way you lead. But I have an important
question: Are you motivated to lead? Ha! I know that is a silly
question, so let me ask, Why are you motivated to lead?

I am thoroughly convinced that great leadership comes
from the heart—a servant leader's heart. I've written two
books on servant leadership, building off spiritual perspectives,
and Robert Greenleaf, who coined the term *servant leader*.[1]
According to Greenleaf, a servant-first leader is focused on a
person's highest priority needs.

Servant leaders, and the best situational leaders, are
focused on the needs of the people they lead. As Susan has
described in this book, motivation science has empirically
validated people's highest priority needs: choice, connection,
and competence—the psychological needs required for them
to flourish. Your leadership capacity to help people fulfill their
basic needs is essential if you want them to produce results and
thrive.

But the best leaders also understand their motivational
outlook for leading—their why. They find meaning by aligning

their leadership decisions and actions to developed values. They integrate their work with a noble purpose. They find inherent joy in positively influencing people's lives and contributing to society.

You make a difference as a leader. What kind of difference will you make? If you put the ideas from this book into action, you will have a better chance of being a servant leader rather than a self-serving one.

Amazon's Hall of Fame inducted Ken Blanchard as one of the top twenty-five best-selling authors of all time. He and Susan have coauthored three books together.[2]

Notes

Foreword

1. Motley Fool, "3 Stocks Warren Buffett Can't Buy."

Introduction

1. Murayama et al., "Undermining Effect of Monetary Reward"; Kerr, Feltz, and Irwin, "To Pay or Not to Pay?"
2. Kohn, *Punished by Rewards*; Pink, *Drive*; Fowler, *Why Motivating People Doesn't Work* and *Master Your Motivation*.
3. Ryan and Deci, "Self-Determination Theory"; Deci and Ryan, *Handbook of Self-Determination Research*; Deci and Ryan, "Facilitating Optimal Motivation."
4. Kleinginna and Kleinginna, "Categorized List."
5. Deci et al., "On the Benefits of Giving."
6. Baard, "Intrinsic Need Satisfaction"; Deci and Ryan, *Handbook of Self-Determination Research*; Gagne and Deci, "Self-Determination Theory"; Deci and Ryan, "Facilitating Optimal Motivation."

Chapter 1

1. "Beane Happy to Run A's through 2008."
2. Spectrum of Motivation model is the registered trademark of Mojo Moments Inc., 2023.
3. Moller et al., "Financial Motivation."
4. Moller et al., "Financial Motivation."
5. Moller et al., "Financial Motivation"; Kennedy, "Firms Bet Money."

6. Kovach, "Why Motivational Theories Don't Work."

7. Ryan and Deci, *Self-Determination Theory*; Deci and Ryan, "Facilitating Optimal Motivation"; Kasser, *High Price of Materialism*; Gagne and Deci, "Self-Determination Theory"; Murayama et al., "Undermining Effect of Monetary Reward"; Kerr, Feltz, and Irwin, "To Pay or Not to Pay?"

8. Ryan and Deci, *Self-Determination Theory*; Deci and Ryan, "Facilitating Optimal Motivation"; Kasser, *High Price of Materialism*; Gagne and Deci, "Self-Determination Theory"; Murayama et al., "Undermining Effect of Monetary Reward"; Kerr, Feltz, and Irwin, "To Pay or Not to Pay?"

9. Himesh's story is from a letter to the author, 2014.

Chapter 2

1. Ryan and Deci, *Self-Determination Theory*.

2. Patall, Cooper, and Robinson, "Effects of Choice"; Radel et al., "Restoration Process."

3. Deci et al., "Need Satisfaction, Motivation, and Well-Being"; Gagne and Deci, "Self-Determination Theory."

4. Berinato, "Shut Up Already."

5. Irwin, Feltz, and Kerr, "Silence Is Golden"; Kerr, Feltz, and Irwin, "To Pay or Not to Pay?"

6. Irwin, Feltz, and Kerr, "Silence Is Golden"; Kerr, Feltz, and Irwin, "To Pay or Not to Pay?"; interview with Dr. Irwin, November 2013.

7. Fehr and Renninger, "Samaritan Paradox."

8. Christakis and Fowler, *Connected*.

9. Tay and Diener, "Needs and Subjective Well-Being"; Milyavskaya et al., "Balance across Contexts."

10. See chapter 5 for the definition of *psychological sense*.

11. Vansteenkiste, Ryan, and Soenens, "Basic Psychological Need Theory."

12. Over the past fifteen years, there's been an explosion of academic research validating the importance of self leadership and proactive behavior, including the following: Chia and Parker, "Thinking and Acting in Anticipation"; Konradt, Andreßen, and Ellwlart, "Self-Leadership in

Organizational Teams"; Manz et al., "Serving One Another"; Marques-Quinteiro and Curral, "Goal Orientation"; Neck and Houghton, "Two Decades of Self-Leadership Theory."

Chapter 3

1. Ryan and Deci, "Ego Depletion to Vitality"; Deci and Ryan, "Facilitating Optimal Motivation."

2. Definition by Susan Fowler; copyright 2022, Mojo Moments.

3. Ayduk et al., "Regulating the Interpersonal Self"; Vohs and Baumeister, *Handbook of Self-Regulation.*

4. Mischel, Ebbesen, and Zeiss, "Cognitive and Attentional Mechanisms"; Mischel, Shoda, and Rodriguez, "Delay of Gratification"; Schlam et al., "Preschoolers' Delay of Gratification."

5. Kidd, Palmeri, and Aslin, "Rational Snacking."

6. Gillet et al., "Impact of Organizational Factors."

7. Brown and Ryan, "Benefits of Being Present"; Brown, Ryan, and Creswell, "Mindfulness"; Brown and Holt, "Experiential Processing"; Jenkins and Tapper, "Resisting Chocolate Temptation"; Ryback, "Neurology of Mindfulness."

8. Hitlin and Piliavin, "Values."

9. Garfield, *Peak Performers.*

Chapter 4

1. De Smet et al., "The Great Attrition."

2. Deci and Flaste, *Why We Do What We Do*, 34–36.

3. Conlin, "Popular Management Theories Decoded."

4. Fowler, "Maslow's Hierarchy"; Maslow, *Motivation and Personality*; McClelland, *Human Motivation*; McClelland and Boyatzis, "Leadership Motive Pattern."

5. Zigarmi et al., *The Leader Within*, 174.

6. Huyghebaert et al., "Psychological Safety Climate."

7. Hardré and Reeve, "Training Corporate Managers."

8. Frankl, *Man's Search for Meaning.*

9. Ability InterBusiness Solutions, "Six Japanese Words."; Robson, "50 Eskimo Words."

10. Zigarmi and Nimon, "A Cognitive Approach."

11. Zigarmi and Nimon, "A Cognitive Approach."

12. Four Paws, "Bans on Circuses."

13. Dweck, *Mindset*, 53.

14. Zigarmi et al., *The Leader Within*.

15. Pohnl, "Magic Johnson."

16. The solution to the Two Jugs riddle: the jugs were full of frozen cubes of lemonade and milk. They stayed separate even when poured into the one large vat.

Chapter 5

1. Genovese, "Great Resignation."

2. Caminiti, "How the Great Resignation"; Tanzi, "Millions of Americans Regret"; Botros, "What Is 'Quiet Quitting'?"; De Smet et al., "The Great Attrition."

3. De Smet et al., "The Great Attrition."

4. Fowler, *Master Your Motivation*. This book teaches individuals the skill of motivation. Also see the resources section for learning experiences that teach individuals how to identify their motivational outlook, shift to an optimal outlook, and reflect on their motivation to maintain optimal motivation over time.

5. Zaidleppelin, "On quiet quitting." Notice how Zaid's explanation for quiet quitting discounts the five intentions of employee work passion described in chapter 4.

6. Stillman, "Want to Hang onto Veteran Employees?"

7. Akhtar, "WeWork's CEO."

8. Cerullo, "Elon Musk."

9. Chris Wollerman, interview with author, February 2022.

10. De Smet et al., "The Great Attrition"; Alexander et al., "What Employees Are Saying."

11. The author originally changed the *M* in the SMART goal-setting acronym in 1990 while working as the lead developer of the Ken Blanchard Companies' Situational Self Leadership product line, now called Self Leadership. The acronym stands for specific and measurable,

motivating, attainable, relevant, and timebound and trackable. The acronym was subsequently changed in the SLII product line.

12. Ryan and Deci, *Self-Determination Theory.*

13. Kasser, *High Price of Materialism.*

14. Sheldon et al., "Independent Effects of Goal Contents."

15. Andrews, "Stephen Curry."

16. Lush, *Neuroscience of Better Feedback.*

17. Vansteenkeete, Ryan, and Soenens, "Basic Psychological Need Theory."

18. Dweck, *Mindset,* 176–177, 136–137.

19. Plass, Mayer, and Homer, *Handbook of Game-Based Learning.*

20. Witkowski, "Videogames Are a Bigger Industry"; Fandom, "Highest-Grossing Video Game"; Whitten, "'Avatar' Returns."

21. Scott Rigby, Richard Ryan, and Edward Deci, interview with author, 2014.

22. KIRO News Staff, "FBI Offering $10K Reward"; Tillman and Roth, "FAA."

23. Footprint Foundation, "U.S. Bans at a Glance."

24. Heath and Heath, *Power of Moments.*

25. Rousseau et al., "Not So Different After All."

26. Findings are cited with permission from L. Taylor Peyton, Drea Zigarmi, and Mattias Dahlgren from an interview with the author, November 13, 2022.

27. Mayer, Davis, and Schoorman, "An Integrative Model."

28. Peyton, Zigarmi, and Fowler, "Basic Psychological Needs"; Orsini and Rodrigues, "Supporting Motivation"; Tang, Cai, and Zhang, "Paternalistic Leadership."

29. Peyton, Zigarmi, and Fowler, "Basic Psychological Needs"; Bartholomew et al., "Self-Determination Theory."

30. Kellerman, *Bad Leadership.*

31. Zigarmi et al., "Beyond Engagement."

32. Zigarmi et al., "Employee Work Passion Model."

33. Zigarmi and Nimon, "A Cognitive Approach"; Hagger, Chatzisarantis, and Harris, "Psychological Need Satisfaction."

34. Used with permission by Drea Zigarmi, Susan Fowler, and Mojo Moments, Inc., from research and white paper in process.

35. Shuck, Roberts, and Zigarmi, "Employee Perceptions"; Shuck, Zigarmi, and Owens, "Psychological Needs."

Chapter 6

1. Amber Barnes, interview with author, August 2022.
2. Beth Scalone, interview with author, July 2022.
3. Brock Weatherup, interview with author, September 2022.
4. Karen Adams, interview with author, August 2022.
5. Mike Easley, interview with author, 2014 and August 2022.

Chapter 7

1. Kovach, "Why Motivational Theories Don't Work."
2. Ken Blanchard, interview with author, 2014.
3. Zigarmi et al., *Leadership-Profit Chain*.
4. Drea Zigarmi, interview with author, 2014 and September 2022.
5. Peyton, Zigarmi, and Fowler, "Examining the Relationship."
6. Peyton, Zigarmi, and Fowler, "Examining the Relationship."
7. Ken Blanchard, interview with author, 2014 and September 2022.

Chapter 8

1. Dweck, *Mindset*.

Afterword

1. Greenleaf, "The Servant as Leader."
2. Blanchard and Fowler-Woodring, *Empowerment*; Blanchard, Fowler, and Hawkins, *Self Leadership and the One Minute Manager*; Blanchard, *Leading at a Higher Level*.

Bibliography

Ability InterBusiness Solutions. "Six Japanese Words That Describe Rice."
Ability InterBusiness Solutions (blog), July 30, 2019. a-ibs.com/en
/blog/article/six-japanese-words-that-describe-rice.html.

Akhtar, Allana. "WeWork's CEO Said People Who Are Most Comfortable
Working from Home Are the 'Least Engaged' with Their Job." *Business
Insider*, May 12, 2021. businessinsider.com/wework-ceo-least-engaged
-workers-comfortable-wfh-2021-5.

Alexander, Andrea, Aaron De Smet, Meredith Langstaff, and Dan Ravid.
"What Employees Are Saying about the Future of Remote Work."
McKinsey, April 1, 2021. mckinsey.com/capabilities/people-and
-organizational-performance/our-insights/what-employees-are
-saying-about-the-future-of-remote-work.

Andrews, Malika. "Stephen Curry Details What Makes His 4th Title
Different from the Others | NBA Today." ESPN, June 17, 2022.
YouTube video. youtube.com/watch?v=YOn4dKTA5RM.

Ayduk, O. N., R. Mendoza-Denton, W. Mischel, G. Downey, P. K. Peake,
and M. L. Rodriguez. "Regulating the Interpersonal Self: Strategic
Self-Regulation for Coping with Rejection Sensitivity." *Journal of
Personality and Social Psychology* 79, no. 5 (2000): 776–792.

Baard, Paul P. "Intrinsic Need Satisfaction in Organizations: A
Motivational Basis of Success in for-Profit and Not-for-Profit Settings."
In *Handbook of Self-Determination Research*, edited by Edward L.
Deci and Richard M. Ryan, 255–275. Rochester, NY: University of
Rochester Press, 2002.

Bartholomew, K. J., N. Ntoumanis, R. M. Ryan, J. A. Bosch, C.
Thogersen-Ntoumani. "Self-Determination Theory and Diminished
Functioning: The Role of Interpersonal Control and Psychological
Need Thwarting." *Personality and Social Psychology Bulletin* 37, no. 11
(2011): 1459–1473.

"Beane Happy to Run A's through 2008." *Sports Illustrated*, November 11, 2002.

Berdrow, Iris, and Frederick T. Evers. "Competence: Bases for Employee Effectiveness." In *Handbook of Human Resource Development*, edited by Neal E. Chalofsky, Tonette S. Rocco, and Michael Lane Morris, 201–214. Hoboken, NJ: John Wiley, 2014.

Berinato, Scott. "If You Want to Motivate Someone, Shut Up Already." *Harvard Business Review* 91, no. 7 (July/August 2013): 24–25.

Blanchard, Kenneth H. *Leading at a Higher Level: Blanchard on Leadership and Creating High Performing Organizations*. Upper Saddle River, NJ: FT Press, 2009.

Blanchard, K. and S. Fowler-Woodring. *Empowerment: Achieving Peak Performance through Self-Leadership*. Escondido, CA: Blanchard Family Partnership/Successories, Inc., 1998.

Blanchard, Kenneth H., Susan Fowler, and Laurence Hawkins. *Self Leadership and the One Minute Manager: Increasing Effectiveness through Situational Self Leadership*. New York: William Morrow, 2005.

Botros, Alena. "What Is 'Quiet Quitting'? Gen Z Is Ditching Hustle Culture to Avoid Burnout." *Fortune*, August 14, 2022.

Bronkhorst, Quinton. "Games vs. Movies: Who Wins?" *BusinessTech*, August 14, 2012. businesstech.com/news/general/19901/games-vs-movies-who-wins/.

Brown, K. W., J. D. Creswell, and R. M. Ryan. *Handbook of Mindfulness: Theory, Research, and Practice*. New York, NY: Guilford Press, 2015.

Brown, Kirk W., and Melissa Holt. "Experiential Processing and the Integration of Bright and Dark Sides of the Human Psyche." In *Designing the Future of Positive Psychology: Taking Stock and Moving Forward*, edited by Kennon M. Sheldon, Todd B. Kashdan, and Michael F. Steger, 147–159. New York: Oxford University Press, 2011.

Brown, Kirk W., and Richard M. Ryan. "The Benefits of Being Present: Mindfulness and Its Role in Psychological Well-Being." *Journal of Personality and Social Psychology* 84, no. 4 (2003): 822–848.

Brown, Kirk W., Richard M. Ryan, and J. David Creswell. "Mindfulness: Theoretical Foundations and Evidence for Its Salutary Effects." *Psychological Inquiry* 18, no. 4 (2007): 211–237.

Burnette, J. L., E. M. VanEpps, E. J. Finkel, E. H. O'Boyle, and J. M. Pollack. "Mind-Sets Matter: A Meta-analytic Review of Implicit Theories and Self-Regulation." *Psychological Bulletin* 139, no. 3 (2013): 655–701.

Caminiti, Susan. "How the Great Resignation Could Turn into the Great Employee Return." CNBC Workforce Wire, August 17, 2022. cnbc

.com/2022/08/17/how-the-great-resignation-could-turn-into-the
-great-employee-return.html.

Cerullo, Megan. "Elon Musk Says Remote Work Is 'No Longer
Acceptable.'" CBS News, June 2, 2022. cbsnews.com/news/elon
-musk-tesla-remote-work-return-to-office/.

Chalofsky, N. E., T. S. Rocco, and M. L. Morris, eds. *Handbook of Human
Resource Development*. Hoboken, NJ: John Wiley, 2014.

Christakis, Nicholas A., and James H. Fowler. *Connected: The Surprising
Power of Our Social Networks and How They Shape Our Lives—How
Your Friends' Friends' Friends Affect Everything You Feel, Think, and Do*.
New York: Back Bay Books, 2011.

Conlin, Bennett. "Popular Management Theories Decoded." Business.
com, June 2017. business.com/articles/popular-management
-theories-decoded/.

Csikszentmihalyi, Mihaly. *Flow: The Psychology of Optimal Experience*.
New York: Harper Perennial Modern Classics, 2008.

De Smet, Aaron, Bonnie Dowling, Bryan Hancock, and Bill Schaninger.
"The Great Attrition Is Making Hiring Harder. Are You Searching
the Right Talent Pools?" McKinsey, July 13, 2022. mckinsey.com
/capabilities/people-and-organizational-performance/our-insights
/the-great-attrition-is-making-hiring-harder-are-you-searching-the
-right-talent-pools.

Deci, Edward L., and Richard Flaste. *Why We Do What We Do*. New York:
G. P. Putnam's Sons, 1995.

Deci, E. L., J. G. La Guardia, A. C. Moller, M. J. Scheiner, and R. M. Ryan.
"On the Benefits of Giving as Well as Receiving Autonomy Support:
Mutuality in Close Friendships." *Personality and Social Psychology
Bulletin* 32, no. 3 (March 2006): 313–327.

Deci, Edward L., and Richard M. Ryan. "The Importance of Universal
Psychological Needs for Understanding Motivation in the Workplace."
In *The Oxford Handbook of Work Engagement, Motivation, and Self-
Determination Theory*, edited by M. Gagne, 13–32. New York, NY:
Oxford University Press, 2014.

Deci, Edward L., and Richard M. Ryan. "Facilitating Optimal Motivation
and Psychological Well-Being across Life's Domains." *Canadian
Psychology* 49, no. 1 (2008): 14–23.

———, eds. *Handbook of Self-Determination Research*. Rochester, NY:
University of Rochester Press, 2002.

Deci, Edward. L., R. M. Ryan, M. Gagne, D. R. Leone, J. Usunov, and
B. P. Kornazheva. "Need Satisfaction, Motivation, and Well-Being

in the Work Organizations of a Former Eastern Bloc Country: A Cross-Cultural Study of Self-Determination." *Personality and Social Psychology Bulletin* 27, no. 8 (August 2001): 930–942.

Dweck, Carol. *Mindset: The New Psychology of Success.* New York: Ballantine Books, 2007.

Edmonds, Chris, and Lisa Zigarmi. *#Positivity at Work Tweet Book 01: 140 Bite-Sized Ideas to Help You Create a Positive Organization Where Employees Thrive.* Cupertino, CA: THINKaha, 2012.

Facer, D. C., Jr., F. Galloway, N. Inoue, and D. Zigarmi. "Creation and Initial Validation of the Motivation Beliefs Inventory: Measuring Leaders' Beliefs about Employee Motivation Using Four Motivation Theories." *Journal of Business Administration Research* 3, no. 1 (January 2014): 1–18. sciedu.ca/journal/index.php/jbar/article/view/3905.

Fandom. "List of Highest-Grossing Video Game Franchises." *Fandom,* Video Game Sales, accessed September 24, 2022. vgsales.fandom. com/wiki/List_of_highest-grossing_video_game_franchises.

Fehr, Ernst, and Suzann-Viola Renninger. "If We Live in a Dog-Eat-Dog World, Then Why Are We Frequently So Good to Each Other? The Samaritan Paradox." *Scientific American Mind* 14, no. 5 (2004): 15–21.

Footprint Foundation. "U.S. Bans at a Glance." Footprint Foundation, accessed September, 24, 2022. footprintusfoundation.org/single -use-plastic-legislation.

Four Paws. "Bans on Circuses." Four Paws in US, accessed September 24, 2022. fourpawsusa.org/campaigns-topics/topics/wild-animals /worldwide-circus-bans.

Fowler, S. "Toward a New Curriculum of Leadership Competencies: Advances in Motivation Science Call for Rethinking Leadership Development." *Advances in Developing Human Resources* 20, no. 2 (2018): 182–196.

Fowler, S. *Master Your Motivation: Three Scientific Truths for Achieving Your Goals.* San Francisco, CA: Berrett-Koehler, 2019.

Fowler, S. "What Maslow's Hierarchy Can't Teach You about Motivation." *Harvard Business Review,* November 26, 2014.

Frankl, Viktor E. *Man's Search for Meaning.* Boston: Beacon Press, 2006.

Gagne, M. ed. *The Oxford Handbook of Work Engagement, Motivation, and Self-Determination Theory.* New York, NY: Oxford University Press, 2014.

Gagne, M., and A. Panaccio. "The Motivational Power of Job Design." In *The Oxford Handbook of Work Engagement, Motivation, and Self-Determination Theory,* edited by M. Gagne, 165–180. New York, NY: Oxford University Press, 2014.

Gagne, M., E. Chemolli, J. Forest, and R. Koestner. "A Temporal Analysis of the Relation between Organizational Commitment and Work Motivation." *Psychologica Belgica* 48, no. 2–3 (2008): 219–241.

Gagné, Marylene, and Edward L. Deci. "Self-Determination Theory and Work Motivation." *Journal of Organizational Behavior* 26 (2005): 331–362.

Garfield, Charles. *Peak Performers: The New Heroes of American Business.* New York: William Morrow, 1987.

Genovese, Daniella. "The Great Resignation Turns to the Great Regret as Worker Needs Are Not Being Met, Expert Says." Fox Business, August 9, 2022. foxbusiness.com/lifestyle/great-resignation-great-regret -worker-needs-not-being-met.

Gillet, Nicolas, Evelyne Fouquereau, Jacques Forset, Paul Brunault, and Philippe Columbat. "The Impact of Organizational Factors on Psychological Needs and Their Relations with Well-Being." *Journal of Business Psychology* 27 (2012): 437–450.

Greenleaf, Robert K. "The Servant as Leader." The Greenleaf Center for Servant Leadership, 1970.

Gunnell, K. E., P. R. E. Crocker, P. M. Wilson, D. E. Mack, and B. D. Zumbo. "Psychological Need Satisfaction and Thwarting: A Test of Basic Psychological Needs Theory in Physical Activity Contexts." *Psychology of Sport and Exercise,* 14 (2013): 599–607.

Hardré, P. L., and J. Reeve. "Training Corporate Managers to Adopt a More Autonomy-Supportive Motivating Style Toward Employees: An Intervention Study." *International Journal of Training and Development,* 13 (2009): 165–184.

Hagger, Martin S., Nikos L. D. Chatzisarantis, and Jemma Harris. "From Psychological Need Satisfaction to Intentional Behavior: Testing a Motivational Sequence in Two Behavioral Contexts." *Personality and Social Psychology Bulletin* 32, no. 2 (February 2006): 131–148.

Heath, Chip, and Dan Heath. *The Power of Moments.* New York: Simon & Schuster, 2017.

Hitlin, Steven, and Jane A. Piliavin. "Values: Reviving a Dormant Concept." *Annual Review of Sociology* 30 (2004): 359–393.

Howe, Neil, and William Strauss. *Generations: The History of America's Future, 1584 to 2069.* Fort Mill, SC: Quill, 1992.

Huei Wu Chia, and Sharon K. Parker. "Thinking and Acting in Anticipation: A Review of Research on Proactive Behavior." *Advances in Psychological Science* 21, no. 4 (2013): 679–700.

Huyghebaert, T., N. Gillet, F-J. Lahiani, A. Dubois-Fleury, and E. Fouquereau. "Psychological Safety Climate as a Human Resource Development Target: Effects on Workers Functioning through Need Satisfaction and Thwarting." *Advances in Developing Human Resources* 20, no. 2(2018): 169–181.

Irwin, Brandon C., Deborah L. Feltz, and Norbert L. Kerr. "Silence Is Golden: Effect of Encouragement in Motivating the Weak Link in an Online Exercise Video Game." *Journal of Medical Internet Research* 15, no. 6 (2013): 1–10.

Jackson, Phil, and Hugh Delehanty. *Sacred Hoops: Spiritual Lessons of a Hardwood Warrior*. New York: Hyperion Books, 2006.

Jackson, Phil, and Hugh Delehanty. *Eleven Rings: The Soul of Success*. New York: Penguin Press, 2013.

Jenkins, Kim T., and Katy Tapper. "Resisting Chocolate Temptation Using a Brief Mindfulness Strategy." *British Journal of Health Psychology* 19, no. 3 (September 2013): 509–522.

Kasser, Tim. *The High Price of Materialism*. Chester, NJ: Bradford Book Company, 2003.

Kellerman, Barbara. *Bad Leadership: What It Is, How It Happens, Why It Matters*. Boston: Harvard Business Press, 2004.

Kennedy, Kelly. "Firms Bet Money Will Prod Employees to Health." *USA Today*, November 25, 2011.

Kerr, Norbert L., Deborah L. Feltz, and Brandon C. Irwin. "To Pay or Not to Pay? Do Extrinsic Incentives Alter the Kohler Group Motivation Gain?" *Group Processes and Intergroup Relations* 16, no. 2 (2012): 1–12.

Kidd, Celeste, Holly Palmeri, and Richard N. Aslin. "Rational Snacking: Young Children's Decision-Making on the Marshmallow Task Is Moderated by Beliefs about Environmental Reliability." *Cognition* 126, no. 1 (2013): 109–114.

KIRO News Staff. "FBI Offering $10K Reward in Commercial Aircraft Laser Incidents near SEA." KIRO 7, April 4, 2022.

Kleinginna, Paul R., Jr., and Anne M. Kleinginna. "A Categorized List of Motivation Definitions, with a Suggestion for a Consensual Definition." *Motivation and Emotion* 5, no. 3 (1981): 263–291.

Kohn, Alfie. *Punished by Rewards: The Trouble with Gold Stars, Incentive Plans, A's, Praise, and Other Bribes*. 2nd ed. Boston: Mariner Books, 1999.

Konradt, Udo, Panja Andreßen, and Thomas Ellwart. "Self-Leadership in Organizational Teams: A Multilevel Analysis of Moderators and

Mediators." *European Journal of Work and Organizational Psychology* 18, no. 3 (2009): 322–346.

Kotsou, I., J. Gregoire, M. Mikolajczak, and D. Nelis. "Emotional Plasticity: Conditions and Effects of Improving Emotional Competence in Adulthood." *American Psychological Association* 96, no. 4 (2011): 827–839.

Kovach, Kenneth. A. "Why Motivational Theories Don't Work." *Society for Advancement of Management* 45, no. 2 (Spring 1980): 54–59.

Kremer, W., and C. Hammond. "Abraham Maslow and the Pyramid That Beguiled Business." *BBC News Magazine*, September 2013. BBC.com /news/magazine-23902918.

Langer, E. J. *Mindfulness*. Reading, MA: Addison-Wesley, 1989.

Lush, Georgia. *The Neuroscience of Better Feedback—Empower, Evolve, and Excel Together*. Improve NLI Webinar. NeuroLeadership Institute. 2016. neuroleadership.com/portfolio-items/improve-feedback -july2017/.

Manganelli, L., A. Thibault-Landry, J. Forest, and J. Carpentier. "Self-Determination Theory Can Help You Generate Performance and Well-Being in the Workplace: A Review of the Literature." *Advances in Developing Human Resources* 20, no. 2 (2018): 227–240.

Manz, C. C., B. C. Skaggs, C. L. Pearce, and C. L. Wassenaar. "Serving One Another: Are Shared and Self-Leadership the Keys to Service Sustainability?" *Journal of Organized Behavior* 36, no. 4 (2015): 607–612.

Marques-Quinteiro, Pedro, and Luís Alberto Curral. "Goal Orientation and Work Role Performance: Predicting Adaptive and Proactive Work Role Performance through Self-Leadership Strategies." *Journal of Psychology* 146, no. 6 (2012): 559–577.

Maslow, W. A. *Motivation and Personality*. New York, NY: Harper, 1954.

Mayer, R. C., J. H. Davis, and F. D. Schoorman. "An Integrative Model of Organizational Trust." *Academy of Management Review* 20, no. 3 (1995): 709–734.

McClelland, D. C. *Human Motivation*. Glenview, IL: Scott Foresman, 1985.

McClelland, D. C., and R. E. Boyatzis. "Leadership Motive Pattern and Long-Term Success in Management." *Journal of Applied Psychology*, 67, no. 6 (1982): 737–743.

Meyer, John P., and Marylene Gagne. "Employee Engagement from a Self-Determination Theory Perspective." *Industrial and Organizational Psychology* 1, no. 1 (2008): 60–62.

Milyavskaya, Marina, I. Gingras, G. Mageau, R. Koestner, H. Gagnon, J. Fang, and J. Boiche. "Balance across Contexts: Importance of Balanced Need Satisfaction across Various Life Domains." *Personal Social Psychology Bulletin* 35, no. 8 (2009): 1031–1045.

Mischel, Walter, Ebbe B. Ebbesen, and Antonette R. Zeiss. "Cognitive and Attentional Mechanisms in Delay of Gratification." *Journal of Personality and Social Psychology* 21, no. 2 (1972): 204–218.

Mischel, Walter, Yuichi Shoda, and Monica L. Rodriguez. "Delay of Gratification in Children." *Science* 244, no. 4907 (May 26, 1989): 933–938.

Moller, A. C., H. G. McFadden, D. Hedeker, and B. Spring. "Financial Motivation Undermines Maintenance in an Intensive Diet and Activity Intervention." *Journal of Obesity* 2012 (2012): 1–8.

Motley Fool. "3 Stocks Warren Buffett Can't Buy." Motley Fool, August 15, 2017. fool.com/investing/2017/08/15/3-stocks-warren-buffett-cant-buy-but-you-can.aspx.

Murayama, K., M. Matsumoto, K. Izuma, and K. Matsumoto. "Neural Basis of the Undermining Effect of Monetary Reward on Intrinsic Motivation." *Proceedings of the National Academy of Sciences of the United States of America* 107, no. 49 (October 2010): 1–6.

Neck, C. P., and J. D. Houghton. "Two Decades of Self-Leadership Theory and Research: Past Developments, Present Trends, and Future Possibilities." *Journal of Managerial Psychology* 21, no. 4 (2006): 270–295.

Nimon, K., and D. Zigarmi. "The Work Cognition Inventory: Initial Evidence of Construct Validity for the Revised Form." *Journal of Career Assessment* 21, no. 3 (February 12, 2014): 117–136.

Orsini, C., and V. Rodrigues. "Supporting Motivation in Teams Working Remotely: The Role of Basic Psychological Needs." *Medical Teacher* 42, no. 7 (2020): 828–829.

Page, Kathryn M., and Dianne A. Vella-Brodrick. "The 'What,' 'Why' and 'How' of Employee Well-Being: A New Model." *Social Indicators Research* 90 (2009): 441–458.

Patall, Erika A., Harris Cooper, and Jorgianne C. Robinson. "The Effects of Choice on Intrinsic Motivation and Related Outcomes: A Meta-analysis of Research Findings." *Psychological Bulletin* 134, no. 2 (2008): 270–300.

Peyton, T., D. Zigarmi, and S. N. Fowler. "Basic Psychological Needs and Need Thwarting as Mediators between Forms of Perceived Leader Controlling Behaviors, Organizational Politics, Hard/Soft Forms

of Power, Trust, and Employee Work Intentions." Oral presentation
at the 6th International Conference on Self-Determination Theory
in Victoria, British Columbia, Canada, June 2016.

————. "Examining the Relationship between Leaders' Power Use,
Followers' Motivational Outlooks, and Followers' Work Intentions."
Frontiers in Psychology 9, no. 2620 (2019).

Pink, Daniel H. *Drive: The Surprising Truth about What Motivates Us.* New
York: Riverhead Books, 2011.

Plass, Jan L., Richard E. Mayer, and Bruce D. Homer, eds. *Handbook of
Game-Based Learning.* Cambridge, MA: MIT Press, 2020.

Pohnl, Elliott. "Magic Johnson, Wayne Gretzky and 13 Great Players Who
Couldn't Coach." *Bleacher Report,* November 17, 2010. bleacherreport
.com/articles/520877-magic-johnson-wayne-gretzky-and-13-great
-players-who-couldnt-coach.

Radel, R., P. Sarrazin, L. G. Pelletier, and M. Milyavskaya. "Restoration
Process of the Need for Autonomy: The Early Alarm Stage." *Journal of
Personality and Social Psychology* 101, no. 5 (2011): 919–934.

Reeve, Johnmarshall. *Understanding Motivation and Emotion.* 5th ed.
Hoboken, NJ: Wiley, 2008.

Reio, T. G., and L. C. Batista, Jr. "Psychological Foundations of HRD."
In *Handbook of Human Resource Development,* edited by Neal E.
Chalofsky, Tonette S. Rocco, and Michael Lane Morris, 1–20.
Hoboken, NJ: John Wiley, 2014.

Rigby, Scott C., and R. M. Ryan. "Self-Determination Theory in
Human Resource Development: New Directions and Practical
Considerations." *Advances in Developing Human Resources* 20, no. 2
(2018): 133–147.

Rigby, Scott C., and Richard Ryan. *Glued to Games: How Video Games
Draw Us In and Hold Us Spellbound.* Santa Barbara: Praeger, 2011.

Robson, David. "There Really Are 50 Eskimo Words for 'Snow.'"
Washington Post, January 14, 2013. washingtonpost.com/national
/health-science/there-really-are-50-eskimo-words-for-snow/2013
/01/14/e0e3f4e0-59a0-11e2-beee-6e38f5215402_story.html.

Rock, David. *Your Brain at Work: Strategies for Overcoming Distraction,
Regaining Focus, and Working Smarter All Day Long.* New York: Harper
Business, 2009.

Rodriguez, D., R. Patel, A. Bright, D. Gregory, and M. K. Gowing.
"Developing Competency Models to Promote Integrated Human
Resource Practices." *Human Resource Management* 41, no. 3 (2002):
309–324.

Rousseau, Denise M., Sim B. Sitkin, Ronald S. Burt, and Colin Camerer.
    "Not So Different After All: A Cross-Discipline View of Trust."
    Academy of Management Review 23, no. 3 (1998): 393–404.
Ryan, Richard M., Jessey H. Bernstein, and Kirk W. Brown. "Weekends,
    Work, and Well-Being: Psychological Need Satisfactions and Day of
    the Week Effects on Mood, Vitality, and Physical Symptoms." *Journal
    of Social and Clinical Psychology* 29, no. 1 (2010): 95–122.
Ryan, Richard M., and James P. Connell. "Perceived Locus of Causality
    and Internalization: Examining Reasons for Acting in Two Domains."
    Journal of Personality and Social Psychology 57, no. 5 (1989): 749–761.
Ryan, R. M., and E. L. Deci. *Self-Determination Theory: Basic Psychological
    Needs in Motivation, Development, and Wellness*. New York, NY:
    Guilford Press, 2017.
———. "From Ego Depletion to Vitality: Theory and Findings Concerning
    the Facilitation of Energy Available to the Self." *Social and Personality
    Psychology Compass* 2, no. 2 (2008): 702–717.
———. "Self-Determination Theory and the Facilitation of Intrinsic
    Motivation, Social Development, and Well-Being." *American
    Psychologist* 55, no. 1 (January 2000): 68–78.
Ryback, David. "Self-Determination and the Neurology of Mindfulness."
    Journal of Humanistic Psychology 46, no. 4 (October 2006): 474–493.
Schlam, T. R., N. L. Wilson, Y. Shoda, W. Mischel, and O. Ayduk.
    "Preschoolers' Delay of Gratification Predicts Their Body Mass 30
    Years Later." *Journal of Pediatrics* 162, no. 1 (2013): 90–93.
Sheldon, Kennon, Richard M. Ryan, Edward L. Deci, and Tim Kasser.
    "The Independent Effects of Goal Contents and Motives on Well-
    Being: It's Both What You Pursue and Why You Pursue It." *Personality
    and Social Psychology Bulletin* 30, no. 4 (April 2004): 475–486.
Shippmann, Jeffery S., Ronald A. Ash, Mariangela Batjtsta, Linda Carr,
    Lorraine D. Eyde, Beryl Hesketh, Jerry Kehoe, Kenneth Pearlman,
    Erich P. Prien, and Juan I. Sanchez. "The Practice of Competency
    Modeling." *Personnel Psychology* 53, no. 3 (September 2000):
    703–740.
Shuck, B., D. Zigarmi, and J. Owens. "Psychological Needs, Employee
    Engagement, and Work Intentions: A Bayesian Multi-Measurement
    Mediation Approach and Implications for HRD." *European Journal of
    Training and Development* 39, no. 1 (2015): 2–21.
Shuck, B., T. P. Roberts, and D. Zigarmi. "Employee Perceptions of the
    Work Environment, Motivational Outlooks, and Employee Work

Intentions: An HR Practitioner's Dream or Nightmare?" *Advances in Developing Human Resources* 20, no. 2 (February 2018): 1–17.

Skinner, B. F. *The Behavior of Organisms: An Experimental Analysis.* New York: Appleton-Century, 1938.

Skinner, B. F. *Walden Two.* New York: Macmillan Company, 1948.

Smith, J. Walker, and Ann Clurman. *Generation Ageless.* New York: HarperCollins, 2007.

Stillman, Jessica. "Want to Hang onto Veteran Employees? Now's the Time for Retention Raises, Says Adam Grant." *Inc.*, June 8, 2022. inc.com/jessica-stillman/employee-compensation-retention-raises -adam-grant.html.

Tang, R., Y. Cai, and H. Zhang. "Paternalistic Leadership and Subordinates' Trust in Supervisors: Mediating Effects of Basic Psychological Needs Satisfaction." *Frontiers in Psychology* 12 (August 2021).

Tanzi, Alexandre. "Millions of Americans Regret the Great Resignation." *Bloomberg*, July 12, 2022. bloomberg.com/news/articles/2022-07-12 /millions-of-americans-regret-quitting-in-the-great-resignation.

Tay, Louise, and Ed Diener. "Needs and Subjective Well-Being around the World." *Journal of Personality and Social Psychology* 101, no. 2 (2011): 354–365.

Thibault-Landry, A., Egan, R., Crevier-Braud, L., Manganelli, L., and Forest, J. "An Empirical Investigation of the Employee Work Passion Appraisal Model Using Self-Determination Theory." *Advances in Developing Human Resources* 20, no. 2 (2018).

Tillman, Rachel, and Samantha-Jo Roth. "FAA: Laser Incidents Targeting Airplanes on Track for Another Record-Breaking Year." *Spectrum News NY1*, May 12, 2022.

Vansteenkiste, M., R. M. Ryan, and B. Soenens. "Basic Psychological Need Theory: Advancements, Critical Themes, and Future Directions." *Motivation and Emotion* 44 (2020): 1–31. doi.org/10.1007/s11031 -019-09818-1.

Vohs, Kathleen D., and Roy F. Baumeister. *Handbook of Self-Regulation: Research, Theory, and Applications.* 2nd ed. New York: Guilford Press, 2013.

Whitten, Sarah. "'Avatar' Returns to Theaters as Disney Tries to Hype Audiences for Its Long-Delayed Sequel." CNBC, September 22, 2022. cnbc.com/2022/09/22/avatar-returns-theaters-disney-hypes-way-of -water.html.

Witkowski, Wallace. "Videogames Are a Bigger Industry Than Movies and North American Sports Combined, Thanks to the Pandemic." *Marketwatch*, January 2, 2021. marketwatch.com/story/videogames -are-a-bigger-industry-than-sports-and-movies-combined-thanks-to -the-pandemic-11608654990.

Zaidleppelin. "On quiet quitting #workreform." Tik Tok, July 25, 2022. tiktok.com/@zaidleppelin/video/7124414185282391342.

Zigarmi, Drea, Kenneth H. Blanchard, Michael O'Connor, and Carl Edeburn. *The Leader Within: Learning Enough about Yourself to Lead Others Within*. Upper Saddle River, NJ: FT Press, 2004.

Zigarmi, Drea, Scott Blanchard, Vickie Essary, and Dobie Houson. *The Leadership-Profit Chain*. Escondido, CA: Ken Blanchard Companies, 2006.

Zigarmi, Drea, Susan Fowler, and Dick Lyles. *Achieve Leadership Genius*. Upper Saddle River, NJ: Financial Times Prentice Hall, 2008.

Zigarmi, Drea, and K. Nimon. "A Cognitive Approach to Work Intention: The Stuff That Employee Work Passion Is Made Of?" *Advances in Human Resources Development* 13, no. 4 (2011): 443–457.

Zigarmi, Drea, K. Nimon, D. Houson, D. Witt, and J. Diehl. "Beyond Engagement: Toward a Framework and Operational Definition for Employee Passion." *Human Resource Development Review* 8, no. 3 (2009): 300–316.

———. "A Preliminary Field Test of an Employee Work Passion Model." *Human Resource Development Quarterly* 22, no. 2 (2011): 195–221.

Zigarmi, Drea, and Taylor P. Roberts. "Leader Values as Predictors of Employee Affect and Work Passion Intentions." *Journal of Modern Economy and Management* 1, no. 1 (2012): 1–32.

Zigarmi, D., T. P. Roberts, and B. Shuck. "Motivation and Internal Frames of Reference: Do We Have the Wisdom to Help Employees Flourish at Work?" *Advances in Developing Human Resources* 20, no. 2 (2018): 127–132.

Resources

Are you optimally motivated to continue your learning journey and share it with others? These learning resources will support your leadership capacity to master motivation with others. You'll also discover resources for learning motivation as a skill—the perfect companion for co-creating optimal motivation with the people you lead.

Keynotes and Consulting

You can book Susan Fowler and Mojo Moments thought leaders for keynote presentations, workshops, or consulting by inquiring at Info@MojoMoments.com.

Susan's Books

You can find Susan's books online and in bookstores, including

- *Master Your Motivation*
- *Achieve Leadership Genius*, with Drea Zigarmi and Dick Lyles
- *Leading at a Higher Level*, with Ken Blanchard and colleagues

- *Self Leadership and the One Minute Manager*, with Ken Blanchard and Laurence Hawkins

Mojo Moments Learning Experiences and Resources

Mojo Moments is a global consulting and training community of channel partners and strategic alliances that provide scientifically sound and field-tested solutions, products, and services that transform leaders and organizations. Mojo Moments learning experiences are embraced globally by Fortune 500 companies and midsize to small-size businesses, government agencies, and educational and nonprofit organizations.

Known for its cutting-edge and empirically based Spectrum of Motivation model, Mojo Moments is dedicated to improving psychological sense for leaders and individuals at all levels of the organization.

Contact Mojo Moments at Info@MojoMoments.com for information about learning experiences, products, e-books, and white papers on topics supporting the ideas in this book, including the following:

- Mastering your motivation
- Mastering motivation with others
- Motivational outlook conversations
- Rethinking leadership now that everything else has changed
- Leading yourself
- DISCovering self and others
- Giving and receiving optimal feedback

- High-quality goal setting
- Leadership in context
- Trust
- Employee work passion
- Leading authentically

Visit Mojo Moments' website for free surveys, white papers, blog posts, podcasts, videos, information on becoming a channel partner or strategic alliance, and additional resources at MojoMoments.com.

Mojo Movement

Join our Mojo Movement to gain access to robust online conversations and learning opportunities, receive our CHOMP Newsletter, or become a channel partner or strategic alliance partner. Reach out to Susan at Susan.Fowler@MojoMoments .com.

Acknowledgments

When I was young, I would stand in front of the mirror using my hairbrush as a pretend microphone and deliver my Academy Award speech for winning Best Documentary. In my fantasy, the orchestra played me off the stage because I took too long thanking all my collaborators. I guess I've always understood the humility of winning—you simply don't do anything worthwhile alone.

These acknowledgments are my humble attempt at expressing gratitude to those who helped evolve the ideas expressed in this book with their support, brilliance, and insight. (If you are missing from this list, forgive me and trust that you are valued.)

Our Mojo Moments core team is foundational to this work. My heartfelt love and gratitude to Alexandra Dinu, Erez Almogi, Judes Donin, Mary Evans, Nikita Wollerman, and Rares Manolescu. A special shout-out to Taylor Peyton's invaluable edits and thought leadership.

We do what we do with optimal motivation because of our partners and dogged collaborators: Drea Zigarmi, Duncan Cork, Paul Donin, Andra Manolescu, Owen Evans, Nancy Biggar, Kathy Ambrose, Jim Diehl, Marina Gabriela Soare, Cosmin Tudora, Aaron Robbins, Kelie Snow, Joakim Hovrevik, Mattias Dahlgren, and Petra Brohall.

Our Legacy Partners spread motivation skills throughout the world. The list is ever growing, but we need to acknowledge the early adapters who shaped the thinking in this book, including Andrew Miedler and Ian Beeson at Blanchard Australia, Viorel Panaite and his team at HumanInvest in Romania, Michal Zaborek and his team at House of Skills in Poland, Anna Kirin and her team at CBSD in Russia, Tao Wang and 51Job in China, Robert Van Den Bergh from Blanchard International in the Netherlands, Erez Amolgi and Blanchard Israel, Marie Segura at CMC Business Solutions in the Philippines, Amber Barnes at StartHuman in Nevada, Jimmy Karam and Aaron Robbins at IntrinsicFirst in San Diego, Jean-Paul Richard at Tangible Performance in Quebec, Dave Cordery at AKTAA in New Zealand, Richard Gilmore at SEAC in Thailand, John McNulty and People Focus Consulting in Japan, Alvar Piera and Jose Crespo Solans with Beckman Coulter, Joe Hepsworth and Wavetronix, Paula Daoust with Blue Cross Blue Shield of Kansas, and Chris Freund and Max Scheichenost with their team from Mekong Capital in Vietnam.

I've been blessed with colleagues, friends, and family who aided and perhaps suffered through the development of these ideas, especially Els Kaelen, Maria Pressentin, Jason Arnold, Lynn Hutton, Chris Wollerman, Mattias Borg, Marty Gilbert, Mark Paskowitz, Bulent Levi, Yogesh Sood, Philippe Mailleux, Seval Özcan, Morgan Pierse, Antony Demetriou, Marija Pavic, Spiros Paolinelis, David Facer, Jenny Luna, Gary Onstad, Trudy Panchon, Kip Fowler, and the Del Vecchio, Talbert, Fogoros and Creighton clans.

I am forever grateful to the Ken Blanchard Companies for their early support of the ideas expressed in this book, especially Richard Pound, Ken Blanchard, Jay Campbell, and Victoria Cutler.

Most of the stories in this book are attributed to values-based clients past and present who embraced optimal motivation and helped me learn more than I taught. If I didn't mention them by name in honor of NDAs, you know who you are!

Behind the scenes, these people made this book a reality:

- *Berrett-Koehler Publishers*—The reason this book exists, Neal Maillet. The man behind BK's values, Steve Piersanti; copy editor extraordinaire, Sharon Goldinger; and our shepherd, Jeevan Sivasubramaniam. The production and marketing teams, foreign rights group, and the BK Author Community, who support and inspire in equal measure.
- *My PR team at Weaving Influence*—Becky Robinson, Aubrey Pastorek, and Izzy Thornton.
- *The master of science in executive leadership program at the University of San Diego*—Our students, faculty, and amazing team for a robust learning lab over the past twenty years.
- *My work heroes in the Self-Determination Theory community*—Edward Deci, Richard Ryan, Jacques Forest, Marylène Gagné, Scott Rigby, and the extraordinary Shannon Hoefen Cerasoli.

Many years ago, my forever partner, Drea Zigarmi, asked me, "What's the penny you want to leave the world?" My answer was to translate complex motivation science into practical application so people worldwide could experience optimal motivation, thrive, and live their lives at a higher level. The penny on the dedication page is in his honor. Thanks to his love and wisdom, this work exists, and *my* life has been elevated to a higher level.

Index

About the Author

Susan Fowler is the founder and CEO of Mojo Moments, an international organization represented by channel partners and strategic alliances who recognize that motivation is at the heart of everything people do—and everything they don't do but wish they did.

Susan is on a quest to help leaders at all levels flourish as they succeed. Widely known as one of the foremost experts on motivation and personal empowerment, she gained her knowledge through extensive experience in business, advertising, sales, production, marketing, executive and lifestyle coaching, and leadership training in all fifty states and over forty foreign countries. Susan has worked with clients as diverse as AkzoNobel, Apple, Bayer, Bloomberg, Google, Harley-Davidson, Inspire Software, Merrill Lynch, Moody's, National Basketball Association, Pfizer, TJ Maxx, and Wavetronix.

The first edition of *Why Motivating People Doesn't Work . . . and What Does* became a bestseller translated into fourteen languages. Susan's *Master Your Motivation* is a companion book teaching individuals the skill of motivation. She is the lead developer of the Ken Blanchard Companies' Self Leadership program and coauthor of three books with Ken Blanchard: *Self Leadership and the One Minute Manager*, *Leading at a Higher Level*, and *Empowerment*. Susan has produced the audio programs *Overcoming Procrastination* and *Mentoring* and coauthored *Achieve Leadership Genius* with Drea Zigarmi. She was awarded the Lifetime Achievement Award for instructional design by the North American Simulation and Gaming Association.

Susan lives with her husband, Drea Zigarmi, in San Diego. Communicate with her at Susan.Fowler@MojoMoments.com and MojoMoments.com. Connect with Susan on social media:

Facebook: @SusanNFowler
Twitter: @fowlersusann
LinkedIn: Susan Fowler
Instagram: @susannfowler

Berrett–Koehler
Publishers

Berrett-Koehler is an independent publisher dedicated to an ambitious mission: *Connecting people and ideas to create a world that works for all.*

Our publications span many formats, including print, digital, audio, and video. We also offer online resources, training, and gatherings. And we will continue expanding our products and services to advance our mission.

We believe that the solutions to the world's problems will come from all of us, working at all levels: in our society, in our organizations, and in our own lives. Our publications and resources offer pathways to creating a more just, equitable, and sustainable society. They help people make their organizations more humane, democratic, diverse, and effective (and we don't think there's any contradiction there). And they guide people in creating positive change in their own lives and aligning their personal practices with their aspirations for a better world.

And we strive to practice what we preach through what we call "The BK Way." At the core of this approach is *stewardship,* a deep sense of responsibility to administer the company for the benefit of all of our stakeholder groups, including authors, customers, employees, investors, service providers, sales partners, and the communities and environment around us. Everything we do is built around stewardship and our other core values of *quality, partnership, inclusion,* and *sustainability.*

This is why Berrett-Koehler is the first book publishing company to be both a B Corporation (a rigorous certification) and a benefit corporation (a for-profit legal status), which together require us to adhere to the highest standards for corporate, social, and environmental performance. And it is why we have instituted many pioneering practices (which you can learn about at www.bkconnection.com), including the Berrett-Koehler Constitution, the Bill of Rights and Responsibilities for BK Authors, and our unique Author Days.

We are grateful to our readers, authors, and other friends who are supporting our mission. We ask you to share with us examples of how BK publications and resources are making a difference in your lives, organizations, and communities at www.bkconnection.com/impact.

Dear reader,

Thank you for picking up this book and welcome to the worldwide BK community! You're joining a special group of people who have come together to create positive change in their lives, organizations, and communities.

What's BK all about?

Our mission is to connect people and ideas to create a world that works for all.

Why? Our communities, organizations, and lives get bogged down by old paradigms of self-interest, exclusion, hierarchy, and privilege. But we believe that can change. That's why we seek the leading experts on these challenges—and share their actionable ideas with you.

A welcome gift

To help you get started, we'd like to offer you a **free copy** of one of our bestselling ebooks:

www.bkconnection.com/welcome

When you claim your **free ebook**, you'll also be subscribed to our blog.

Our freshest insights

Access the best new tools and ideas for leaders at all levels on our blog at ideas.bkconnection.com.

Sincerely,

Your friends at Berrett-Koehler